FRONTIERS IN AMERICAN CATHOLICISM

FRONTIERS IN AMERICAN CATHOLICISM

Essays on Ideology and Culture

by WALTER J. ONG, S.J.

The Macmillan Company, New York, 1961

Macmillan Paperbacks Edition 1961

The Macmillan Company, New York
Brett-Macmillan Ltd., Galt, Ontario

Printed in the United States of America

ACKNOWLEDGMENTS

"Renaissance Humanism and the American Catholic Mind" was one of the McAuley Lectures given at St. Joseph College, West Hartford, Connecticut. "American Catholicism and America" and "Renaissance Ideas and the American Catholic Mind" appeared in separate issues of THOUGHT (XXVII, 521–41; XXIX, 327–56), copyright 1952, 1954 by Fordham University. "Contrasts in Catholicism" was originally printed in COMMONWEAL (LXIII, 9, pp. 215–19), copyright 1955 by Commonweal, Inc.
For permission to publish these essays, grateful acknowledgment is hereby made to the holders of the original copyright.

IMPRIMI POTEST
D. H. Conway, S.J.
Provincial, Missouri Province
St. Louis, Missouri, October 30, 1955

IMPRIMATUR
✠ Joseph E. Ritter
Archbishop of St. Louis
St. Louis, Missouri, November 10, 1955

Library of Congress catalog card number: 57-5730

In Memory of
My Father and Mother

INTRODUCTION

THESE ESSAYS HAVE developed as attempts to think through and explain some of the many problems with which American Catholicism is faced today, particularly those along the ideological front. Some of the problems are being faced by Catholicism elsewhere, too, but all of them present some particular urgency in the United States. The essays have been written in various places—Paris, London, Boston, St. Louis—and under the kindly stimulation of a great number of friends, American and foreign.

This is an age when men across the world are becoming more and more conscious of cultural pluralism and of the importance of cultural perimeters, past, present, and future, for the development of man and his work in the universe. We are struck by the fact that activity, and often the most important and significant activity, takes place along lines of division or quasi-division—where an old culture meets a new, or where the business world impinges on the intellectual, or where the "inner-directed" impulse engages "other-directedness." American Catholicism exhibits a great many perimeters of all sorts. For this reason it is being studied both by Americans and by others, whether Catholic or not, with growing interest. The present book is the product of such interest in American Catholicism as a phenomenon with varied perimeters or frontiers.

The range of these essays is somewhat wide, the reason being that, because of the pluralism of the society in which it exists, the American Catholic consciousness is stirred by currents deriving from unexpected and often distant sources. It has become a commonplace that Americans are, in a special but profound sense, more complex psychologically than Europeans. American culture is in great part European culture transplanted and compelled to reform its fronts of activity, and that not by forgetting its past experiences —this is impossible—so much as by drawing on them to adjust itself to a new world as well as to a certain infusion of other cultures.

Because the culture of the United States has so many of its roots outside the United States, this country often serves as a kind of proving ground or point of focus for certain global problems, including those particular problems faced by present-day Christians. For example, the need for a Christian humanism of this technological era to which the evolution of the cosmos has currently brought mankind is a particularly urgent need in the United States. Here the world frontier is peculiarly an American frontier, and for this reason a treatment of this important problem is included in the present volume.

Of these six essays, the first has appeared in *Thought*, the second in *Études* (Paris—in French version), the third in *Commonweal*, and the fourth, given at Saint Joseph College, West Hartford, Connecticut, in slightly different form as a lecture honoring Mother Mary Catherine McAuley, in *The McAuley Lectures, 1954*.

W. J. O., S.J.

Saint Louis University
March 25, 1956

CONTENTS

1

THE AMERICAN CATHOLIC COMPLEX

In a discussion of what we may call the things of the spirit in America, it is well to recall that there is a very real sense in which these things today, all over the world, are much the same. An intellectual evolution, implemented by and itself spurring on the material evolution of the means of communication, has made of our planet a psychological whole today in a way it was never a psychological whole before. As Father Pierre Teilhard de Chardin has brought home at least to Frenchmen, happenings in Paris, London, Tokyo, Washington, Rome, and—with reservations—Moscow, are present not only in these various places, but simultaneously and uninterruptedly in the minds of millions all over the world, so that the collective human consciousness has a common fund now, not of history alone but of actuality, which is completely new in the story of the human race.

A community of interest is especially marked between Europe and America, for these two great sections of humanity have not only a common present but a common past. This is true especially of the United States (and likewise of Canada), where the native Indian cultures had not reached the development they reached south of the Rio Grande and have left only relatively slight traces on the transplanted European sensibility. Europe will always be the past out of which the United States emerged, just as the United States is largely a shoot of Europe grown out into the future.

Where reality is experienced as the whole weight of the past—

literary, philosophical, historical—comes to bear on the present, the similarity between Europe and the United States of America is most marked. This is the intellectual front, and, despite some divergence of interests, to any twentieth century "intellectual," whether he is European or American, this front is for the most part the same.

If a community of interests is manifested in a general way for all human beings of the present day, it is doubly manifest for present-day Catholics, who live in a tradition capable of penetrating indifferently all cultures, and, indeed, designed by God to do precisely this. A study of American Catholicism can therefore very profitably take the form of a study of the continuity of this Catholicism with the rest of the world. Europeans know this approach to American Catholicism—perhaps too well. They avail themselves instinctively of explanations of American Catholicism cast in terms of its old nationalistic European backgrounds. But such explanations can be badly bungled for want of a real knowledge of what these backgrounds mean *in America*. When they talk, as they talk incessantly, about the Irish tradition in American Catholicism, Europeans can fail to see the fact that this tradition does not so much directly determine the character of American Catholicism as afford a meeting point for the general American tradition and the Church in America. There is a curious affinity, which I do not pretend to explain, between the hail-fellow-well-met Irish friendliness and the cordiality of the larger American tradition which has its roots in the frontier. The Irish tradition is less a determinant than a catalyst. The American often hears the European identify as Irish things which he knows have a much larger range.

But the American Catholic cannot very gracefully object to the European's lack of understanding, for the American Catholic has been able to explain himself to himself and to others no better than the European spectator can explain him. He has no explicit theory to fit his case, and he has shown relatively few signs of developing one —until recent times. For now American Catholicism is in a state of intellectual and spiritual crisis. It is becoming self-conscious, and an American Catholic conception of the mission of the Church in

America, seen precisely as America, is beginning to take more definite form.

Not that American Catholicism has had no vision of history before. The American Catholic has always carried deep in his consciousness a set of notions which made him feel himself engaged in history in a very definite way. His vision of himself in history has been the product of two forces: the post-Revolutionary period of nineteenth century Catholicism in which most American Catholics came to America, and the minority, defensive position in which the Church found itself in a culture which really, although never quite officially, was anti-Catholic. Both forces built up within the American Catholic consciousness the strong minority mentality and intellectual squints so often remarked. The immediate reaction to a hostile environment was not to understand it, but to resist it. The result has been a paradox still puzzling to foreigners: a Catholic mentality which in many ways is the most conservative in the world set in the midst of the nation whose genius seems to be adaptability and change.

It is out of this defense mentality that the American Catholic consciousness as a whole has drawn its notion of its position in history. I say the Catholic consciousness as a whole, for, when it comes to individual American Catholics, many can be found whose views are set in a much wider framework. Like all views of history, that of the American Catholic consciousness has been projected back out of a real situation as a reflection of real psychological needs. All history is mythmaking, not in the sense that it creates what did not exist—if it does this, it is simply not history—but in the sense that from the agglomerate of the past it pulls out clusters of items which are symbolically rich and psychologically helpful at the time the history is being written. It drops out of its picture—history always and necessarily drops out more than it puts in—what it finds "uninteresting," which means what it finds has no symbolic relevance to the present instant. It erects a view of the past which, however true, is selective. The selection favored by American Catholicism has been determined by the fact that this Catholicism was not only faced with the general run of nineteenth century attacks on the Church but with the additional threat of the predominantly anti-Catholic, although, in the large, curiously benign, Protestant culture of the United States in which it was making its home.

The minority complex of American Catholics has been often enough commented upon, but it is not always noted that this complex is involved not only with the status of the Church in America but with a certain historical perspective developed by American Catholics and occasioned not at all by their minority condition in America but more simply by the fact that they are both Catholics and Americans. This double heritage of theirs generates in them a curious sense of their mission. First, Europe becomes for them, as for all Americans, a symbol of the past. Second, because this past is psychologically and geographically severed from the moving present, which to Americans is necessarily America, it becomes invested with a quiescence or even rigidity greater than most pasts ordinarily have. To an American, the past tends to be something left behind —Land's End or Cape Finisterre abandoned beyond the horizon. It loses some of its normal condition as a component of the present.

Even to a European in Europe, the past may seem to be a series of stationary points. The human condition is such that we tend so to think of the past. But the European has evidence of a fluid past all around him. He can see the forward movement of history asserting itself in an architectural monument which is a hodgepodge of successive styles reduced to harmony by a sense of construction full of compromise with time and shifts in style. He can see Gothic architecture coming into being in the hybrid and graceful inconsistencies of Saint-Germain-des-Prés. For the American, Gothic is the less lovely St. Patrick's Cathedral, soaring futilely into the flanks of skyscrapers, put together all at once in an unconvincing unity which seeks to freeze this copy of the past outside all real time. Nineteenth century Europe gave birth to similar imitation Gothic, it is true—and this fact only reminds us again of the similarity of the American and European sensibility. But in America this is all there is of the past: only imitations—which, be it noted, make much more sense in America than in Europe as externalizations of the past which the American is already carrying around in his soul and which would otherwise have nothing at all outside to relate itself to.

Thus far, the American Catholic is like every other American in erecting Europe into a symbol of the past and in suffering from the fact that this symbol makes the past more static for him than it does for a European. But at this point, the American Catholic comes face to face with a difficulty all his own. It is from somewhere within this past that the Faith has come. With this past, this series of spastic poses, continuity must be preserved. The resulting vision for an American Catholic can be very disquieting. He finds himself committed as a Catholic to a past whose static quality his own American situation has exaggerated for him. Other Americans can dismiss their concept of the past with a horse laugh, as Mark Twain does in *A Connecticut Yankee in King Arthur's Court*. Or they can, with more sophistication, see it as something "rich, deep, and dark," but as somehow distinct from themselves, as Henry James's Americans do, or as Henry James himself did, taking up residence in England somewhat as a connoisseur might set up housekeeping in an art gallery. The American Catholic's attitude is more complex because it is less detached.

Thus it is that American reliance on Europe as a source of vitality in culture becomes in the case of American Catholics exaggerated beyond measure. The prizing of translations, with or without reason, over native works; the instinctive deference to the European theorist or lecturer or writer, the assumption that the ultimate intellectual achievement for American Catholicism is to bring to completion an exhaustive raid on what Europeans are saying and to make all this available to the man in the American street—these attitudes are all too evident, not, indeed, in the minds of first-rate American Catholic intellectuals but in what might be called the "well informed" American Catholic mentality.

This mentality surpasses in subservience to Europe anything on the non-Catholic scene. The subservience has many explanations, no one of them adequate alone. There is the inevitable facing toward

Rome, and the tendency to regard those who are geographically closer to the center of Christendom as somehow knowing better what everything is all about. There is the immaturity of American Catholicism itself considered in terms of its age in calendar years. There is the associated fact that American Catholicism has long been preoccupied with getting its bearings, and so has had to practice keeping its eyes on others.

But all these explanations together are inadequate, for, when it comes practically to adapting Catholic life to the actuality of living, American Catholicism does not exhibit this reliance on Europe at all. Back of all these explanations lies the further explanation of the American Catholic's peculiar historical perspective. He is haunted by the notion that in being older, Europe is somehow truer to the Catholic tradition than he is. Europe is the past, from which Catholicism comes, the static past—all this seems obvious but awkward, for he has no working familiarity with the static.

If it is occasionally evident to the American Catholic that Europe is not really always more static than America, if it is in European Catholic circles rather than in American that the virtues of the "historical sense" are extolled, or if it is in Europe that the new Catholic intellectual fronts form—to some extent, says the American Catholic consciousness to itself, it is natural that Europeans have something to do with activity. Theirs is a special function here. They know how to stabilize the new currents, to arrest them and thus to make them safe. The worker priests, the new liturgical efforts—these things are dangerous, and we shall wait till the Europeans have put them through the experimental stage, immobilized them like the other things we think of in connection with Europe, till the Catholics of Paris and Bordeaux and Brussels and Cologne, those suburbs of the Eternal City, have worked out what is admissible and what is not. Europeans may bristle all they want at this American way of associating them with what is immobilized. They may insist that they have no interest in stabilizing things, that they want to make the innovations *work*. But they have no choice. The Catholics of America have decided that from Europeans they will gain their assurance.

The curious mentality here, to the European puzzling but in the American spontaneous and highly effective, can well be seen in terms of the American Catholic's way of viewing his magnificent educational system. If one can trust his recollection of countless sermons, exhortations, random speechifying, and commencement addresses, United States Catholics regard their heroic and remarkably successful struggle for Catholic education from the lowest through the highest professional levels largely in terms of a recovery effort. They are somewhat encouraged in this by a mentality inherited from post-Reformation British Catholicism. They believe that they are fighting to get back to a system of Christian schooling which somehow or other—the villains are generally the Reformation and Rationalism, rarely modern science—the modern world has lost. The American Catholic writings in the disputes at the close of the past century concerning the respective educational rights of the family, the Church, and the state exhibit a curious mixture of first-hand appreciation of the then current situation in all its complexity together with a tendency to formalize the dispute in such a way as to suggest that the question had all been settled in a static past and that somehow changed conditions had upset an erstwhile Utopia, whereas, as a matter of fact, Catholics were face to face with what was largely a new situation to which no definitive answers had ever been given.

Collectively, American Catholics seem quite unaware that their achievement in setting up their present school system represents not only a remarkable achievement in the face of a neutral state which gives no financial assistance whatsoever to any but state schools, but also a tremendous development in the interior economy of Catholic life itself.

American Catholics speak of their educational "system" and of their parish schools, often enough, as educational "plants," using concepts quite unknown to an earlier world. Quite naturally, for these things are the product of the Church's twentieth century life. Never in the history of Christianity, including the height of the Middle Ages, has the Church as such been charged with an organized educational program which even remotely compares with that in the present United States, with its 3,500,000 elementary school pupils, its nearly 700,000 secondary-school pupils, and its 300,000 students in Catholic universities and other institutions at the university level. The presence of nearly 100,000 women religious—about two-thirds the total number of women religious in the United States—as teachers in this educational system, from the elementary through the university level, is itself a revolutionary phenomenon. The corresponding figure for formal education in medieval times is zero.

The American Catholic feels the success—not perfect by any means, but appreciable—of this education effort. But he seldom feels it as the product of the twentieth century Church in the twentieth century world—as this moment of the Incarnation. In his more thoughtful moments, he feels it as an approximation of the past Utopia. Inevitably, the literary movements to which American Catholic students are alerted are "revivals" or "renascences." All vitality must come out of the past. Every cause must have been dead at least once to appeal to the American Catholic soul.

The American Catholic is likely to hold up to his mind's eye the medieval university as the symbol his educational apparatus is trying to measure up to. He is seldom aware that in so important a thing as the formal teaching of Christian doctrine his educational system, like those of other present-day Catholics in other countries, has far outdistanced the medieval university, where there were not even any catechisms and where the only persons who ever formally studied the content of Christian revelation at all were the tiny handful of specialists following the tedious (twelve-year or longer) theology courses. But that the Church in America has in any way improved on the "age of faith" remains practically unthinkable.

II

If I have made a great deal of the attitude of American Catholicism toward its historic past, this is not because that attitude is very close to the surface of the American consciousness but because it is different from what is at the surface. At the surface of the American Catholic consciousness is a tremendously vital know-how, an ability to keep alive the message of Christ, to keep Christ present in the face of changes which are so far along the trajectory of history that we are assured by Romano Guardini in *Das Ende der Neuzeit* that the word "modern" no longer describes them. In so far as it is vital, American Catholicism is essentially adaptability, an adaptability keeping alive the spiritual, interior message of the Gospel in the present-day industrial world of mass culture, and possible only where the Church is face to face with this world in its concentrated American form.

But there is as yet no intellectual grasp on the part of American Catholics of their real part in the historical process as a historical process—again, I speak in the large, for individual American Catholics are quite aware of the situation we are speaking of here. The general American Catholic consciousness has avoided all but a captious acquaintance with Hegelianism, and has not alerted itself to theories of America as America. History tends to remain a series of stereopticon slides—mostly of Europe—and this in a day when it is a commonplace that the historical sense is a necessary component of any first-rate contemporary awareness, and that thinking today without this component is doomed to ineffectiveness.

There is an obvious discrepancy between this absence of a historical sense and a mode of life which, with some éclat, is living an evolution into the future. This discrepancy has created the vague malaise in present-day American Catholicism. But the malaise is like the malaise of adolescence, full of promise, and rather likely to end in a spurt of productivity.

III

At the practical level, facing into the future means today engagement in one way or another with the mass culture which is the distinctive form of the age of "peoples'" democracies and of such implements of communication as journalism, motion pictures, radio, television, and the advertising and propaganda which go with all these media. United States Catholicism is intimately engaged with this world of mass culture, and its most characteristic gestures are attempts to impregnate it with Christ. The United States is perhaps the only country where subway advertisements invite non-Catholics to follow lecture or correspondence courses in Catholic doctrine and where you can get exact statistics on the effectiveness of this modern application of the principle *fides ex auditu.* The charges urged against Catholicism in the United States—superficiality, mechanization, routine—are exactly the charges which are leveled against mass culture itself, and which are, we are beginning to see, themselves rather superficial charges, based on little understanding of the complexities of frustration and fulfillment which this mass culture brings.

A recent writer on American Catholicism cites as characteristic American developments the social and recreational life which has developed around the parish church in America and "a certain rather superficial optimism" which he finds everywhere in the United States. The two points are well chosen to show the influence of the American milieu on Catholicism, but their implication is not adequately explained. Both are connected with the kind of good-fellowship or "sociability" which characterizes a highly developed industrial culture, and both are related to the problems of personality development which such a culture creates.

The social and recreational activities in the Catholic parish in the United States—from baseball teams to sewing clubs, from bowling leagues to religious study circles—come into being, at the expense of great effort on the part of priests and laymen, because of the group consciousness which is so much a part of the American way of life. Any ruffling of the surface of American life leaves a wake of "organizations" of a semisocial nature after it. Even Masonic lodges, whose activity elsewhere keeps more consistently beneath the surface, in America may well have baseball teams challenging other organizations to competition. Americans go through life in a froth of "organizations," and if the Church does not become present in terms of such organizations she is not very effectively present at all.

The Church's exploitation of the American group consciousness is not limited to parish activity. It is a commonplace that Catholic schools at all levels, elementary to university, are fully integrated in American sports life, with its more or less conscious exploitation of mass loyalties and antagonisms—all in the spirit of "superficial optimism" which characterizes sports generally everywhere today. Explicitly religious organizations ferment into mass movements almost automatically. The Sodality of the Blessed Virgin, originating in Renaissance Europe as an organization of student élite, is engaged in a constant running fight with itself to keep from becoming a mass movement in a milieu where the élite as such enjoys relatively little prestige. In the large, American Catholics and other Americans are not convinced that an élite, in the European sense, is a desideratum in the American milieu, or even, for that matter, that it is a normal condition of existence—a conviction not without immediate beneficial consequences, since it accounts largely for the discredit of the Communist Party, with its peculiarly Central European sense of an élite, in the United States.

It would be foolish to say that there is no élite or no room for an élite in America, but the conditions of existence for an élite are here radically different from what they may be in other cultures. For the Church at present the more effective, or at least the more used, entry into American life has been the spirit of camaraderie or good-fellowship of the classless society—or, as *Fortune* has put it, the society where a permanent revolution reigns. Americans are incredibly vulnerable to this approach. I know personally of a small-town pastor who effectively crippled the anti-Catholicism of the Masonic leaders in his community by a campaign of camaraderie, including a relentless program of handshaking and public cordiality every time he met them on the street. This camaraderie has brought American Catholics not only to become members of the numerous businessmen's lunch clubs which thrive on comradeship and "good will," but to have lunch clubs of their own as well, in which gregariousness is even put to the service of asceticism, as when one of the best known of the Catholic lunch clubs, the Serra Club, modeled in some details on Rotary, sets as its aim the promotion of vocations to the priesthood.

There is, of course, an externalizing momentum in constant traffic with "organization" of one sort or another, just as there is in the methods of advertising, financing, and education employed by American Catholicism, but the momentum is not irreversible. For example, the retreat movement in America is maintained in existence and propagated by a system of circularizing and personal contact (layman-to-layman rather than priest-to-layman) which would do honor to a life insurance agency. But it is largely as a result of this advertising that 300,000 American Catholic laymen made retreats in 1955, in which the noise of the preceding advertising was drowned out by the retreat silence, which is certainly as complete and as deep in an American retreat as it is in retreats elsewhere in the world.

The optimism, "rather superficial," which has been charged against American Catholicism is as typically American as the tendency to become embroiled in a thousand and one organizations. To discount it or to regard it as simply a correlative of material prosperity and a full belly is to reveal a superficial understanding of America. In a certain sense, this optimism is America. It is both a cause and a product of that very real state of mind which students of American literature call "the American dream."

With roots not only in social and economic conditions, but perhaps still more in the euphoria of the American evangelical Protestant and his exhilarating "conviction" of personal salvation, American optimism has real, if equivocal, connections with the Gospel, the "Good News." Psychologically very complex, serving as it does on the one hand actually to build morale and on the other to conceal real feelings, to disguise the tragic and thereby only to make it doubly tragic—as it becomes in *The Death of a Salesman*—this optimism is ineradicable, at least for the present, from the pattern of industrial mass culture which America typifies.

In this culture, "optimism" is oil for the bearings, all the more necessary because of the size and complexity of the mass-culture machine. Nothing strikes an American as more fatuous than the opinion expressed by a recent writer in the Paris daily *Figaro* that France could match American production by copying American methods while eliminating the "rather inane" optimism which characterizes the American industrial world. The "inane optimism" is nothing less than the psychological factor which makes American productivity go, for no one is more aware than American production experts that theirs is not only a problem of machinery but a complex problem of personalities and individual adjustments.

The Death of a Salesman, which is far more a distinctively American tragedy than Theodore Dreiser's long-winded novel, has shown the commonplace personal tragedy which this optimism can hide. But its association with tragedy does not show that the optimism is merely an incident to be eliminated from life. Rather, it shows that it is a part of life, and in a way we are far from completely understanding. The association of the optimism with the figure of a salesman—typical product of industrial culture—reminds us of the connection between this optimism and the art of creating a demand for a supply which shapes all dealings with the masses. American optimism is somehow really tied up with the process of vending —the smile of the pretty girl in the Coca-Cola ad has a deep symbolic value which her designers use without fathoming. It is no accident that the magazine founded in and on this optimism, the *Reader's Digest,* published in its dozens of tongues, turns up in every land on the heels of the industrial mass culture of which America is the typical and purest representative.

The Church's assimilation of the American reality and her transformation of it in accordance with her own mission of sanctification cannot, of course, be uncritical. Indeed, one of the indications of the vigor of the present assimilatory process is precisely the growth in critical effort. A passion for self-criticism and close inspection of the point at which Catholicism and the American way intersect is more and more characteristic of United States Catholicism at its best intellectual and spiritual levels. (Some of the criticism one meets with at other levels is simply a delayed response by Catholics to the wave of self-criticism which swept America between the wars.)

Nevertheless, the critical mentality has not discouraged various plunges into the milieu.

Perhaps most typical of these is the American *Catholic Digest,* spreading out, like its secular counterpart, in various national editions all over the world. The *Catholic Digest* has come off naturally enough, for American Catholic journalism has long been filled with American optimism. Its strong "promotional" tone contrasts, for example, with the more analytical, tongue-in-the-cheek, critical attitude more characteristic of the French Catholic press. The universe of American Catholic pamphlet literature is filled with the same optimism. The attractive presentation and bouncy dialogue of the hundreds of pamphlets by the late and beloved Father Daniel Lord are a famous example of what we might call the mood of optimism exploited for the presentation of Catholic doctrine. Recently, Father James Keller, with his organization of "Christophers" or Christbearers, has built the same optimism into the structure of a national movement which baptizes native American "good will," using it as a common possession of both Catholics and Protestants to expedite the Catholic influence on American life. If virtue goes often unrewarded, the things which encourage it should not, Father Keller believes, and his Christophers offer sizable cash prizes for "constructive" literary works, some of which have been staged and made into real Hollywood motion pictures.

But with all this thoroughgoing exploitation of the ingredients in its milieu, American Catholicism exhibits an almost complete unawareness of the composition and provenance of the ingredients. This unawareness regards not only American optimism and similar components of the American sensibility but even the United States herself as a world-wide psychological fact. With "Americanology" become a full-dress science, the Catholic consciousness remains curiously inert to it all. In Catholic educational institutions, routine courses are given in American literature, but research must be turned on the Middle Ages. Whereas M. Gabriel Marcel has a whole book in French on Josiah Royce's philosophy, it is safe to say that 90 per cent of those who study philosophy in Catholic universities, and many of those who teach it, would not know that Royce was an American, or, for that matter, that he ever existed. They would, however, be under the spell of the milieu which produced him, in the sense that all their lives they would have been making expert use of its possessions.

The Church is Catholic precisely because she is not national in any exclusive sense, and the relative absence of chauvinism among American Catholics, even when they are affected with self-complacency, is undoubtedly welcome, especially in a world launched irrevocably on an international career. Under the leadership of Cardinal Gibbons, Archbishop Ireland, and Bishop Keane, American Catholics spent the past century fighting off one brand of national Catholicism, when the Archangel Raphael Society in Germany, under its secretary Herr Peter Cahensly, was sending memorials to the Holy See about the millions of Catholics (one figure given was 16,000,000!) who had abandoned the faith in America because the American Church pattern did not generally follow national origins in favoring separate German-speaking, Italian-speaking, or other national organization, not only parish but diocesan. It would be a tragedy if American Catholicism, having forgotten even the name of this Cahenslyism, should develop a worse chauvinism of its own, and doubly a tragedy at this stage of history.

But American Catholicism need not be offensive in any nationalistic sense in order to be aware of the components out of which it is made. French Catholicism, one of the most self-aware forms of Catholicism, is notably less chauvinistic than most other aspects of the French national life and character. Chauvinism, the vaunting of one's heritage, and historical awareness of one's heritage are not the same things. For one thing, historical awareness accepts both the good and the bad. Kierkegaard and Heidegger are right in insisting that awareness of and acceptance of one's own personal history is necessary for maturity. This acceptance is the acceptance of the insecurity of the adult, the acceptance of the fact that the individual concrete problems which arise before me have never been settled in the history of the world, although all history brings itself to bear on my settling of them.

A kind of crisis attendant on such acceptance seems to me to be a distinctive mark of the American Catholic consciousness at the present moment. There is no doubt that this acceptance will coincide with a deepening and enriching of the Catholic consciousness in America, for acceptance of one's own history means appropriating the subject matter of that history so as to make it part of one's own inward life, which is enriched accordingly. (We speak always of the general Catholic consciousness, for there is no way to say whether one or another individual American has or has not at present a deeper Catholic consciousness than one or another individual Frenchman or German or Dutchman or Spaniard or Chinese.)

The American Catholic's budding awareness of himself in history is connected with the general increase of awareness on all sides of the place of America in history and with a growing maturity in the Church herself which marks our day. If acceptance of one's own history marks an important step in maturity, whatever her other setbacks, the Church has in this way matured more rapidly in the past few generations than in many centuries before. She has always lived in history, lived the Incarnation out of history into the present, but only with the post-Hegelian interest in history has she become reflexively aware of her mission under this aspect. This awareness involves a more complete acceptance of her own past.

IV

The present intellectual crisis of American Catholicism, as we have described it, has been attended in the past few years by the appearance of the two books of Paul Blanshard, *American Freedom and Catholic Power* and *Communism, Democracy, and Catholic Power*. Blanshard considers the Church as moving toward the ultimate destruction of liberty in America, and, indeed, everywhere in the world. In the second of these books, he attempts a tour de force: the equation of Catholicism and Communism. These books are regarded by Catholics generally as a recrudescence of the mad Protestant anti-Catholicism manifested periodically, if with always decreasing vigor, in various forms of "native Americanism," such as the Ku Klux Klan furor of the twenties. But Blanshard's books are a little more than that. They are the product of the same issues which are producing the crisis in the present-day American Catholic mind: the issues regarding the place of the Church in terms of America's place in history.

Blanshard's attack resembles the work of the historian G. G. Coulton in England. Coulton, approaching history with a personal dislike of the Church verging on the neurotic, adopted a very simple argument, which, indeed, was thrust into his hands by Catholic medievalists—not the professional first-run scholars so much as the popularizers and "semi-pros." You insist, Coulton said, that in the Middle Ages everything was Catholic. I shall go to the Middle Ages, therefore, and show you what you find there—reminding you always that it is all rooted in Catholic culture. And he did. In a similar vein, Blanshard bases his entire attack on the tacit assumption of American Catholics. You wish, he says, to re-create the pattern of the past in America. All right, I shall go to the documents and pronouncements of the past, and see what this pattern will mean. And he does find that, on the basis of the assumptions he can impute to American Catholics, they are only biding their time until they may acquire a majority in America, at which happy time they will establish a police state after the model of Torquemada's or Stalin's, and have done with American liberty, to which they render only lip service.

Blanshard's way of capitalizing on the lack of a well developed historical viewpoint in the American Catholic sensibility as well as his own dull lack of historical sense has, fortunately, occasioned on the Catholic side a plunge into history. Admitting the *de facto* loyalty of Catholics to American democracy, Blanshard has maintained that this loyalty and the principles in papal pronouncements of the past are simply inconsistent with one another. One group of Catholic theologians, following a line of argumentation developed by Dr. John A. Ryan several decades ago, admits the inconsistency, holding that it lodges in the Constitution of the United States itself, which *ought* to say that the American government is obliged to adopt and to profess the Catholic religion (not, of course, to force non-Catholics into the Church),[1] but that, in view of the fact that there is no way of implementing this obligation, Americans are bound to loyalty to their government as it is. By developing an explanation along these lines, this group feels it can preserve the integrity both of Catholic teaching and of the American way of life.

Another group of Catholic theologians adopts a different approach which sees both America and the papal documents in historical contexts and bases itself on the difference between the entity spoken of as the state in earlier papal documents and the entity set up by the American Constitution. In this view, the expression *L'état c'est moi* has some meaning in the mouth of the head of the "state" of earlier times (as well as in some modern societies), for the state was constituted somehow in the *person* of a prince or a king. The czar was the "little Father" of the Russians. But Mr. Eisenhower is in no sense the "great White Father" of American citizens. The President of the United States is essentially an organ of government, not a person acting as such, although the organ is made to function by now this and now that individual. No American ever speaks of or thinks of dying for his President in the way a medieval subject was ready to die for his king. The President is a-personal, and, since worship is the act of a person, the President does not go to the Presbyterian Church. Only Mr. Eisenhower does. The

[1] An excellent account of the issues between the two groups of theologians is that by Gustave Weigel, "The Church and the Democratic State," *Thought*, XXVII (1952), 165–84. Some of the examples here used are borrowed from Father Weigel's account.

question of course remains as to whether the papal documents, in speaking of the only kind of "state" at the time known to men, teach that such a state is the perfect state or the only kind of state ultimately admissible, and that a state organized in the American fashion can only, at best, be tolerated. It would, however, by rather general admission, be quite impossible to show that the papal documents touch this question at all. On the contrary, papal pronouncements from Leo XIII on explicitly praise the American form of government and urge Catholics to loyalty to it.

Thus the latter of the two explanations draws directly on positive papal pronouncements as well as on analytical study. But in its analytical procedure, it shows the historical sense emerging among American Catholics as something urgent to them and emerging at its best—patient, intelligent, and not content with accepting complex issues constituted in the past at their prima facie present-day meaning—not content, that is, to let human thinking develop irresponsibly, as though it were always in full possession of the terms it uses, but insisting that the mind double back constantly over the trail it has pursued to free itself of the contingent more and more, realizing all the time that, being what it is, a mind whose purest abstractions are never angelic but always redolent of the material existences from which they were derived, the human intellect will never in this life be utterly and absolutely the master of its terms. Awareness that there is a history even in the formation of concepts is, again, like all awareness of one's historicity, an exercise in humility and in the acceptance of insecurity. Perhaps it is necessary to remind ourselves that this is not at all the same as relativism. Fundamentally, it is the acceptance not of relativity but of incompleteness.

By the exercise in historicism which it has occasioned, the Blanshard attack is thus more important than many American Catholics are willing to admit—important not in that it will convince other Americans in general that Catholics are conspiring against American liberties, but important in forcing Catholics to a practical realization that there are theological problems raised in terms of the reality which is America for which the answers cannot be found already framed in theology manuals.

When Blanshard chooses as his point of attack the connection between Catholic doctrine and the historical reality which is America, he does so not only because this is the most unattended area along the United States Catholic front but also because he himself has his own very real worries here. Blanshard is fearful of what will happen if Catholic thought becomes as much at home in American culture as Catholic life has already become. He is afraid of the Church's Catholicity, its complete at-homeness in any milieu, its ability to follow the course of history wherever this course may lead. Hence his attack is radically an attempt to immobilize the Church by immobilizing its theory in terms of the past, which his own unimaginative approach invests with a complete rigidity.

In this tactic of immobilization, Blanshard is indeed capitalizing on a real inconsistency in the American Church. But the inconsistency is not between her way of acting and Catholic dogma. It is between her way of acting and her habitual way of thinking about the issues around her. Her activity is well ahead of her theory. Blanshard wants above all that the Church in America act as she has so far tended to theorize: in terms of a deep-frozen European past. If she turns to developing this theorizing in terms of the reality of her life in America, he is lost. And it looks as though that is just what she is on the verge of doing. The signs are many, and one of the most encouraging is the growth of self-aware groups of Catholic intellectuals in Catholic and in non-Catholic universities.

V

Any study pointing up developments in Catholic theology occasioned by the American experience, which is one phase of the experience of the whole human race, will have immediate hearing among the American intellectuals, to whose work American Catholic intellectual activity has hitherto been hardly present. There have been attempts, and very successful ones, to underline the connection between the American way of life and Catholic thinking by bringing out the connection between the tradition which produced the American Constitution and the advanced political theorizing of a Bellarmine or a Suárez. But this is part of the older tendency to base an endorsement of the Church in America once again upon the reduction of an issue to European components. Understandably, such a tendency has a limited appeal to educated Americans who, pretty much in proportion to their education, are already oppressed by a sense of their permanent indebtedness to Europe.

The American intellectual would be much more intrigued by learning what the Church in America has to do with the American experience: with the experience of the frontier, the spirit of enterprise and exploration, the process of expansion; and especially today with the forces at work in a mass, industrialized culture, and with the maintaining and interior development of personality in such a culture. The American intellectual will exhibit an interest in dogma, at times almost frantic, if dogma can be presented to him as historically present, as a deposit of truth which was given by Christ and which subsequently has had a career in the dynamic process of history of which he feels himself a part. There are obvious connections between the dynamic aspects of American life and the theology of mission and of the Incarnation lying at the center of Catholic teaching. Since before the days of the great Cardinal Gibbons, American Catholics have been keen to sense and practically to exploit such affinities. So far, they have had little to offer to the non-Catholic interested in a theological explanation of them.

The one notable, if somewhat rudimentary, theory of Catholicism in the American environment which has appeared to date has two significant aspects or moments. First, it was the product not so much of interest generated in Catholic intellectual circles as it was of interest which took its rise in non-Catholic circles and managed to overcome Catholic apathy. Second, once the theory was moot in Catholic circles, it went the way of most Catholic thinking of the time: it found itself recast in terms of European issues and resolved in the same terms, leaving Americans so chastened by the procedure that they turned more industriously than ever to developing "know-how" and letting theory be.

This whole occurrence took place toward the end of the nineteenth century when a saintly American convert from Protestantism who became the founder of the Paulist Fathers, Isaac Hecker, caught sight of a developing indigenous American Catholicism. Like a contemporary of his, Orestes Brownson, Hecker had come to the Church out of a Protestant milieu of Brook Farmers and Transcendentalists—"harmless charlatans," he called them—alive to the theoretical implications of America in a way Catholics had as yet no time to be. Unlike Brownson's, Hecker's conversion to Catholicism did not release sets of aggressive instincts, for if Father Hecker was to some degree a sanguine enthusiast (and thus a representative American), he was also a sympathetic rather than an aggressive promoter of causes.

He saw Catholicism not as waging war on the American or any other naturally admissible way of life, but as penetrating into the modern world, which he knew principally as it existed in America —"in busy marts, in counting-rooms, in workshops, in homes, and in the varied relations that form human society . . . ; it is into these that sanctity is to be introduced."[2] Father Hecker's interest was abetted by that of the far-sighted Archbishop Ireland of St. Paul, Minnesota, who wrote the Introduction to the life of the Paulist's founder written by Father Walter Elliott.

But Hecker and Ireland were ahead of their times. Neither their nor any other vision of American Catholicism was to be seen consistently in its natural setting. It was first to be reincarnated in Europe, where, in the French translation-adaptation of Father Walter Elliott's *Life of Father Hecker,* it was projected into the highly charged French atmosphere in which were brewing the Integrist squall and other religio-social storms of the Third Republic. Caught in the gusts of controversy, this initial—and, to date, almost sole

[2] Walter Elliott, *The Life of Father Hecker* (New York, 1894), p. 318, quoting Father Hecker.

—theoretical interest in American Catholicism as such was tortured out of shape and accommodated to the old European currents blowing out of the centuries. In the European controversy, a thing styled "Americanism" emerged, described as a kind of muscular Catholicity centered around the exaltation of natural over supernatural virtues. Nothing of Father Hecker's or Archbishop Ireland's was ever condemned, but Leo XIII sent a letter to Cardinal Gibbons which echoed phrases out of the French controversy. The letter blamed no one for anything but presented a positive statement of Catholic doctrine on matters which it noted as under discussion. The theoretical case for American Catholicism, until the past few years, has rested there.

Our understanding of the phenomenon which is America has much advanced since the days of Father Hecker and Archbishop Ireland, and it would be inadvisable to go back to them as "sources." But it is to be hoped that the interest they initiated will in our day be brought to fruition. The problem of the Church in America is simply her age-old problem, always the same and always different—that of spreading the Gospel and thereby of developing the spiritual, that is to say the interiority of mankind, but always under circumstances never quite experienced before.

Only the shallowest of analyses will conclude that this work is more hopeless in our industrial mass culture than it was at times when men, with less domination over material forces, had to spend a greater proportion of their time in struggling with them. That the Church's work will be somewhat different in many external features goes without saying. The very culture we live in enables us to understand and manipulate external techniques with far more address than before. Mankind becomes somehow more self-conscious, more self-possessed as time goes on. This is the inevitable outcome of spiritual existence engaged in material history. It should be the part of American Catholicism—most touched for the present by the external changes—to aid in this self-possession, but in Christ, where alone self reaches fulfillment.

2

AN APOSTOLATE OF THE BUSINESS WORLD

THE ATMOSPHERE OF American business, with its curious mixture of utilitarianism, idealism, optimism, naïveté, and uncanny "know-how" is a seven-days' wonder to the European mind. To the Church in America, this atmosphere is no wonder at all. It is a fact. It is the *donnée* which it is her task to work on, to leaven. There is no question, basically, of praising it or of denouncing it, but of redeeming it.

The American Catholic consciousness knows this world as it knows itself—as something simply there, antecedent to all analysis. If you were to ask an American Catholic today whether there is an apostolate of the business world developing in America, he would probably look as nonplused as Francis of Assisi would have looked if someone had asked him what he proposed to do about evangelizing feudal society. Only later historians are aware in this explicit fashion of "feudal society." For St. Francis there was simply the apostolate of the world around him—the only world he effectively knew. The American apostle of the twentieth century is in much the same situation regarding the American business world of his day.

Thus, without being explicitly aware of it, American Catholics have already succeeded in developing an apostolate of the business and commercial milieu which is, in its own way, unique because it is adapted to the unique situation prevailing in the United States. Europeans have long been aware of this, even if Americans have not always been.

II

Perhaps the most general determinant of the Church's apostolate of the American business world is the complete social acceptability of business in the United States. This social acceptability has made for curious alliances, and none more curious than those between the intellectual and the tycoon. The Church has found in the United States a highly developed speculative approach to commerce. The oldest university in the United States, Harvard University, is probably as famous today for its School of Business Administration as for anything else. In a way quite unknown elsewhere in the world, at American universities and in the technological research programs carried on by the larger business establishments themselves, commerce merges with the study of chemistry, geography, physiology, or—for solving the problems of personal relationships generated by modern industry—with psychology and psychoanalysis.

Faced with a commerce thus carrying academic overtones, the Church has found herself borne by the force of her own educational program into inevitably close relationship with the commercial world. Following a pattern practically unknown in Catholic education outside America, her many universities and still more numerous colleges offer courses in market analysis coupled with courses in ethics, metaphysics, modern languages, or genetics.

The resulting educational program may be kaleidoscopic, dizzying to anyone but Americans, and perhaps to them, too, but it peoples the business world with men of some university background, making for still more contacts between business and university education—again, in a fashion unknown in most places outside the United States. These contacts are still further developed by other specialized schools which, following the almost unique American tradition, are incorporated in American Catholic as in non-Catholic universities—schools such as those of journalism or of industrial relations.

III

The gregariousness of American businessmen has given birth to all sorts of associations primarily commercial in inspiration but rich in noncommercial relations in which the Church has often found openings for her apostolate. This is noteworthy in the case of that typical American institution the lunch club—Kiwanis, the Lions' Club, Rotary, and the like—which serves the cause of camaraderie in a daily round of life which keeps American businessmen away from home for their midday meal.

The Church has not been slow to find that lunch clubs offer her opportunities to make her point of view known and felt, and priests and zealous laymen are naturally happy to be asked to address club members on matters tangent to the Church's life. Indeed, in many instances, speaking before such clubs can become a highly specialized bit of Catholic action undertaken by university students and other groups.

The same Catholics who are making the Church present to other lunch club groups will, of course, also form occasional lunch clubs of their own, such as the Serra Club or various First Friday clubs.

The steps here taken mark a tremendous progress in the life of the Church. Since the Middle Ages, when commerce grew up outside the framework of feudal society as a quasi-illegal activity, the presence of the Church in the world of business has, in many countries, often been regrettably weak. This weakness is closely associated with the weakness of the Church's hold on males. Lunch clubs are predominantly—most often exclusively—masculine organizations, and the Church's penetration of this milieu, like her even more active penetration of the sports world through teams representing various Catholic organizations, educational and other, is really a penetration of the male world as this really exists in the United States. In associating herself here with existing patterns of organization and seeking, however indirectly, to work with them, she is coping with the social intractability of the individual male better, it would seem, than by launching new pious organizations for him which exist only on paper.

IV

The Church's existence in the American commercial world and her growing desire to leaven it with the Gospel have been the result not only of theory flown into the upper story of her educational edifice or of knowledge gained by casual acquaintance over the lunch table. They are also the result of the grim reality of her own daily existence in a thoroughly commercial world. The activity of American Catholicism has, from the start, of necessity been geared to the modern commercial world in the way medieval Catholicism was geared to the feudal system. The material basis of the Church's apostolate in the United States is as fluid as the material basis of the medieval Church was static.

Despite their tremendous annual outlay of money, Catholic institutions in America, including educational institutions from elementary schools through universities, not only receive no state support but are seldom even partially endowed. Often they carry heavy debts. Administrators must have the business acumen not only to spend funds intelligently, but to find them in the first place. Faced with mounting administrative costs, Catholic universities, like other universities, resort to "living endowment" drives, asking those who cannot afford to give, for example, an endowment which would yield a hundred dollars' annual income to pledge themselves to contribute personally a hundred dollars a year instead. Like the "envelope system" of fixed weekly contributions in use in the parishes, this "living endowment" technique shows the Church supporting her exterior activities by promotional methods borrowed from the "going concerns" of the modern commercial world. Business "organization" has replaced the tithe barns of the medieval Church.

At a time when the Church everywhere is more dependent on fluid sources of income than in the past, her condition in the United

States is not unique, save in emphasis. And it must be admitted that endowments are not entirely unknown to the Church in America. But they are relatively rare. Not only financially but psychologically, endowments do not bulk so large as promotional activity. It is no accident that, whereas monsignori, rarities in any other country, are to be found by the hundreds throughout the United States, canons, common enough in other lands, are quite unknown. A canonry suggests an endowed chair, and no one in the United States seems ever to have heard of such a thing. In the give-and-take of a commercial milieu, the concept of establishment corresponds to nothing very compelling.

V

If a sense of movement keeps the Church afloat materially in the sloshing commercial world, it also defines the Church's broader relations with this world in terms of the techniques of mass appeal which modern industry has been most responsible for developing and which, to a superficial foreign observer, constitute the most typically American elements in American Catholicism. However, it is not the means themselves but the Church's attitude toward them that is worth observing.

Radio, television, the posters in the Boston subway announcing the Paulist Fathers' convert classes (for catechumens, but open also to those who want to sit in simply to learn about the Church), the Knights of Columbus' paid advertisements in national magazines offering free Catholic literature to those who send in their names (a parallel with commercial offers), the Catholic Information Society's correspondence course (reminiscent of the long-established commercial correspondence course), the Rosary recited over a nation-wide network by well known practicing Catholics recruited (as for commercial endorsements) from among movie stars—these are techniques which the average American Catholic feels not as means to be used only with a deprecating and pious sigh; they are things which he hopes to see somehow transformed in being used. For they are not techniques laid hold of in a raid executed upon something outside his ordinary consciousness, but rather part of the culture with which he feels most at home and which he wants to redeem through Christ. They are techniques which establish part of his hold on the natural world around him, and his best impulse is, while keeping himself personally detached from them as from all creatures, to drag them and the world of which they are the products to God.

The Church's growing preoccupation with such means is itself indicative of a shifted center of gravity in society. Until recent times it was the state which the Church treated with comparable solicitude, entering into a partnership with it in which she hoped, despite St. Augustine's profound misgivings, by associating its institutions with herself, to drag the state itself to God. As the nations stand before us today, the results of this political apostolate do not appear particularly heartening on the political plane, although the permanent spiritual results of this dialogue with the state are beyond question. Is a new type of dialogue developing? Is it of any significance that in America, where the Church's use of radio and television reaches a kind of apogee and takes on a high symbolic value, these two things are not, as elsewhere, governmental but private commercial enterprises? Is the problem of Church-state alliance being superceded in America by the different problem of Church-business world alliance?

VI

This brings us to the question, Is redemption of the commercial world really possible after all, or even desirable? With the exception of some strongly influenced by the Ruskin-Morris-Gill tradition (and perhaps somewhat by Chesterton), American Catholics on the whole think that it is. In the way, that is, in which such things are said to be redeemed: it can be brought into closer and closer relationship to Christ in terms of the persons involved in it by a process which never reaches its completion here below. The

American Catholic holds this opinion as a practical attitude rather than as a theoretic certainty, for in the United States one will find no developed theology of the redemption of a commercial society at all.

The Catholic's attitude makes itself felt in his reaction to certain phenomena which are typical of the American business world and which have, even there, a vaguely religious coloring. Among these one might single out two, the ideal of "service" and the spirit of "optimism."

The notion of service is associated with the sense of movement inseparable from commerce. In the world of modern business, success turns not merely on corralling static resources, as it might in a feudal society, but also largely on getting something out of one's own hands into the hands of another—for a suitable fee, to be sure, but in an operation which, however base, is inevitably social in bearing. Rotary's motto, "He profits best who serves best," or the gasoline companies' practice of referring to filling stations as service stations may not be altruistic. Indeed, one can detect something quite venal in these devices. Nevertheless, they have a certain social impetus which is positive. The notion of service does confront man with his fellows.

Only an entrenched Jansenism can believe that the social overtones here are so depraved as to be past redemption. Few American priests are Jansenistic, and there is more than one whose motto for the externals of his parish organization, and even for the administration of the sacraments, is frankly "service to the parishioners." The idea needs transformation, yes. But transformation is certainly not impossible or extraordinarily difficult in terms of Isaias' prophecies of the Suffering Servant, Christ, Who came not to be served, but to serve, and Whose Vicar styles himself the Servant of the Servants of God.

The notion of service is closely related to the "optimism" which thrives in the United States. "Service with a smile" runs one of the most popular American mottoes, which has filtered out of the business world to help fix an attitude toward life in general. It is not necessary to remind Americans that this optimism is not philosophic optimism, deriving from a persuasion that this is the best of all possible worlds. Europeans, who are familiar chiefly with this philosophic optimism and are likely to read into American minds theories based on European and not American perceptions, should be wary of thinking that they know just what American optimism is. Basically, this optimism represents no precise philosophical position at all, but rather a studiously cultivated sense of euphoria. It is an emotional attitude marked by a tendency to emphasize the brighter side of things, to fight off feelings of depression, to "keep smiling." It is an effusive and expansive attitude. In the business world, one of its typical manifestations is the conviction that there is no assignable limit to business opportunities, that markets need not remain static but are constantly open to further development, even within territory geographically limited. It is somewhat beside the point to ask if Americans believe in this optimism. It is not a thing you believe in. It is in the air. It is felt. It has its effect, whether you elect to believe in it or not.

This optimism has lent a marked tonality to American Catholicism. It strikes some as ingenuous and childish, as in many of its manifestations it is. But childish or not, it has a not uninteresting history.

Historians point out the connection of this optimism with Evangelical Protestantism. For the Protestant the *élan,* the sense of exaltation and expansiveness, once attaching to religious belief has been transferred to other supports as his dogma has emptied itself of content. It now attaches itself readily to large-scale positive efforts of all sorts, conveying to them a strong moral tonality and a sense of mission.

In a strongly commercial environment, the sense of exaltation attaches to commercial expansion itself. Hence the sense of mission, accompanied by the impulse to "reform" whatever civilization it encounters, which marches with American capitalism around the world. The Coca-Cola representative finds himself a religious enthusiast, an *exalté,* he knows not why—in some places, with his trucks and displays overturned by nativist fanatics, a species of commercial martyr. It is no accident that Mr. and Mrs. De Witt Wallace, creators and owners of the *Reader's Digest,* optimistic traveling companion of modern commercial voyagers and missioner of a cheery do-goodism, are, together with a rather extraordinary number of their early collaborators, children of Protestant ministers.

But the same religious roots which make this optimism deviously Protestant make it also vaguely Catholic. Hence the American Catholic who feels this optimism in his veins feels it as something not to be exorcized, but used. Proposals to do away with this optimism sound to him vaguely irreligious. And the plain fact is that, paradoxically, the Church which must preach Christ crucified has found this optimism one of her most ready points of entry into the American sensibility.

For the same Protestantism which in moments of enthusiastic revivalism can generate an expansive optimism has too grim a theological background to put this optimism to its best use. No matter how strong it may be at a revivalist camp meeting, emotional *élan* is seriously handicapped in a religion which in its day-to-day program, as envisioned by the popular imagination, has laid heavy stress on refraining from alcoholic drinks, from card playing, from smoking, and perhaps even from motion pictures. However far it may actually have moved by today from the old Calvinist concept of God, American Protestantism has unforgettable associations with such a program.

Hence the Protestant has tended to carry his optimism away from his religion into the business world. The Catholic, with a less somber theology, is not so embarrassed by moral negativism. He sees much good, not total depravity, in the natural man, and has always done so as far back as one can go in history. As a manifestation of natural emotion, the optimism generated within Protestantism thus finds a more congenial home, in the long run, in the Catholic Church. Here, beyond the cross, it finds the Resurrection, which for Catholics remains a dogma, not a mere high-sounding word.

VII

Yet, for all her engagement in the American business world and her unselfconscious use there of forces with a more or less Protestant history, the relations of the Church to this business world remain curiously detached. Through the studies of Weber, as qualified by Tawney and later by Fanfani, there is a general awareness today of the "Protestant ethic" which grows up with the modern business world and comes to identify virtue and divine approval with business success. Against this ethic, the reaction of the American Catholic sensibility is immediate, and universally negative. Irvin G. Wyllie explores one manifestation of this ethic in his recent study *The Self-Made Man in America,* and finds Catholicism in the United States noteworthy for its total rejection of any identification of wealth and virtue.

In the wealthiest country of the world at present, there are certainly dangers that Christian poverty of spirit may suffer—although it must always be remembered that wealth is relative, and what might make a man deliriously happy in a late Bronze Age culture might manifest a real spirit of poverty in the United States. Undoubtedly, there are many instances of smugness and hypocrisy in the United States as elsewhere—fine talk about poverty with little inclination to practice it in external things or in spirit. Whether such hypocrisy is a greater danger in the American type of society or in one where there is a greater physical and psychological gap between the rich and the poor is a question which might be studied, but not here.

What is certain is that in the United States, quite as much as elsewhere, poverty, both of spirit and in reality, is portrayed in Catholic teaching as a blessing. Here, as elsewhere, there is the same message to be found in Christ's birth in a stable. The spiritual books are quite at one on this. Whatever abuses there may be, the message of the Church is there, proclaimed by her, clear and piercing, for those who have ears.

This is perhaps one of the minor miracles of our time. That it give rise to tensions is to be expected. The Church in the United States is under no illusions that she can adapt her spirit to the modern business world, or to any other business world. But she feels that she can do something to make her spirit felt in it. Her engagement with the American business complex is not determined by a wish to come to terms with it. But it is a real engagement—spontaneous at the same time that it is wary. The Church feels this milieu is not to be neglected, but redeemed.

3

CONTRASTS IN CATHOLICISM

A RECENT STUDY of the American novel by Marius Bewley has sustained the thesis that the great problem of the serious American novelist has perennially been the relationship of the United States to Europe. This thesis, it seems, can be extended beyond the novel and beyond literature as such. The confrontation of America with Europe has preoccupied the serious American writer because, in one way or another, it tends to become the problem of any serious American mind. To achieve full maturity the American mind must confront itself in its own past, that is, in its own early, pre-American history. This means that it must confront Europe, because Europe is the natural symbol of the past for the American psyche, and that, to a greater or lesser degree, even for those Americans not of European stock.

However, Europe as symbol of the past is not the same thing as Europe of the past. The symbolic Europe which inhabits the American consciousness is felt by this consciousness as something vital. Hence, although it is often actually defined by history-book accounts of a Europe of the past more than by present realities, it is, paradoxically, identified in fact not with this past Europe but rather with the Europe of today, into which the bygone Europe is projected and in which it is felt as still living. The extremes of gushing sentimentality and neurotic revulsion which the sights of Europe can generate in tourists from the United States or which European politics can generate in American public opinion are permanent evidence of the crisis which present-day Europe as a symbol causes in the American soul. Americans cannot react with equal intensity to situations in China or Egypt or even to situations in Texas or Maine or California.

Like other Americans, American Catholics have as a major problem the adjustment of themselves to Europe and to their symbolic image of Europe. Bettering our understanding of the Church in Europe will inevitably help right our understanding of ourselves, so largely governed by what we think Europe is. For this reason, a close examination of European Catholicism, at least in some of its aspects in which American Catholics become emotionally involved, seems in place in a treatment of American Catholic ideology and its adjustment to the world of today. And because the typical American reaction to Europe (like the European reaction to America) is strongest and most rewarding to study where it involves a certain feeling of annoyance, it may be well to select for examination and comparison with the United States a country, Catholic in heritage, with which American Catholics often express some annoyance—namely, France.

II

In the France of the mid-twentieth century, which Père Robert Rouquette of the staff of *Études* has recently suggested in *Thought* is "perhaps the most profoundly Catholic" century in all France's history, the Catholic front presents many mystifying aspects. The aims of the most articulate of French Catholics, which are not always easy even for Frenchmen to explain, are increasingly difficult for foreigners to assess in any meaningful way. Yet it is this very enigmatic character of the French front, and of the French Catholic front, which invites close study. For this enigmatic quality is what particularly annoys many American Catholics by making it increasingly difficult for Americans to avail themselves of Europe as a symbol in any of their favorite ways. To this extent it forces American Catholics to re-evaluate themselves.

Everyone should know that the old landmarks for measuring

the Church's relationship to a changing French culture are no longer serviceable. Practically no one in France hankers for the old union of Church and State. Anticlericalism is so nearly dead that the 1953 "Affaire Finaly"—which, it will be remembered, concerned the sequestering of two children earlier orphaned by Hitler and which lodged some religious in jail—though it was based on real legal issues and not at all trumped-up charges, failed to enkindle any viable anticlerical flames, despite the fact that a few dailies, such as *Franc-Tireur,* did their best to fan the sparks. As in the United States, the great threat to the Faith in France is indifference. But, unlike the situation in the United States, in France, generally speaking, the higher one moves in educational and intellectual circles, the greater the Catholic activity.

Americans know the excellent work of M. Gilson, who is a medievalist, and of M. Maritain, who features medieval insights in his work—for Americans specialize in medievalism. But in other fields at the universities and in the para-university milieu, including the Collège de France, the most competent scholars and scientists include any number of such militant Catholics: MM. Henri-Irénée Marrou, Émile Coornaert, Louis Leprince-Ringuet, Pierre Mesnard, Jean Guitton, Raymond Lebègue, Louis Massignon, Gabriel Marcel, and many others, not to mention occasional priests such as Père Pierre Lejay, S.J., a physicist and member of the Institut, and Père Jean Menasce, O.P., a director of studies at the École des Hautes Études, or theologians of the caliber of Pères de Lubac, Congar, Fessard, Chenu, Daniélou, Bouillard, and others. It is significant that when about four years ago *Figaro littéraire* ran a series of interview-articles on persons whom this most influential of French weekly supplements considered key figures on the intellectual-literary front, the first person written up was Jean-Paul Sartre and the second the late Père Pierre Teilhard de Chardin, the Jesuit anthropologist, credited by another Paris daily with being "the Thomas Aquinas of the twentieth century."

The alteration (for the better) in the Catholic intellectual situation here is paralleled by a shift in other ideological landmarks. The Socialists, avant-garde revolutionaries two generations ago, are now commonly considered by their enemies as ideological fossils—if successful ones, seeing that France, like other Continental countries, is in the long run probably more thoroughly socialized than Great Britain. And the "Radical" Party has recently been labeled reactionary.

Aspects of French Catholicity itself puzzle Americans. American Catholics can become enthusiastic when they are told of the growing number of university students (some ten thousand in 1953) making the annual pilgrimage—the last twenty miles or so on foot —to Our Lady of Chartres. But they cannot understand how this evident devotion can be nurtured in the twentieth century world without courses in apologetics of the sort which American Catholic colleges and universities feature but which are quite unknown at the Institut Catholique (Catholic University faculty) in Paris, Toulouse, or elsewhere. American Catholics are lost when they find that the French apologetic tends to train the youthful mind to think *through* modern problems in Catholic ways, as these problems are being thought through for the first time, and this with a strong stress on familiarity with the Scriptures and with sacramental symbolism rather than on training in epitomes of dogmatic theses, which are regarded as a part of Catholic intellectual life, not as its quasi-totality. In this connection, the American Catholic is likely also to miss in the French mind a sense of a "they" (the scientists) and a "we" (the Catholics interested in apologetics, who know no positive interest in the advance of scientific knowledge but simply lie in wait until the scientists generate a "difficulty" which they can cap with an "answer").

The fact is that a culture as irrevocably Catholic, and as time-scarred, as French culture simply makes for a program of spiritual and intellectual training different from that which American culture demands. The confrontation of the Church and the secular is governed by a different system of ordinates.

III

The system of ordinates is complicated, but some of its salient features can be perhaps re-examined in ways which throw light on American Catholicism itself, by adapting a set of concepts developed by David Riesman in *The Lonely Crowd;* namely, the concepts of the tradition-directed character, the inner-directed character, and the other-directed character.

Riesman's concepts are obviously parallels of the id, the ego, and the superego—I don't know if anyone has called explicit attention to this fact, although I suppose someone has. At any rate, the concepts of tradition-, inner-, and other-directed character seem to appear as correlates of one another and in particular as dialectical-type concepts, generated within an essentially comparative framework, so that the very notion of tradition-directedness generates by reaction inner-directedness, and the resulting interaction generates other-directedness. This is not to say that the interaction of the concepts itself does not apply to reality, for it seems that it does.

Here I shall use the terms in a comparative, interacting framework, applying them in the ways it seems they can be applied to a comparison of French Catholicism with American Catholicism, even though this may entail some modification of Riesman's original notions of the terms.

In this present framework, a tradition-directed character will be taken as one which, by comparison with certain other characters, takes its leads from a pattern of action or attitudes passed on in a society simply as something *given* in the concrete, without much attention to individual achievement or to the development of new solutions to age-old problems. Such a character would be that formed, for example, in a primitive, nonliterate society, where activities such as hunting or various crafts are learned simply by being grown into. Here the pattern of action, and to some extent objectives themselves, are defined by a way of life accepted as part of existence, interior and exterior. In the more primitive tradition-directed societies, there are not even any handbooks or abstract "arts" to guide and form activity and character, only various saws or maxims of very general application.

The Middle Ages can be taken as a representative period when the tradition-directed character in a somewhat more advanced form flourished in the West. In this period we find that, whereas individuals are not discounted as individuals, nevertheless they do not think of themselves as individuals so consciously and explicitly as eighteenth century Europeans or as present-day Europeans and Americans do. There is no literature about individualism in the Middle Ages such as there is today. While a degree of individualism may be tolerated or even encouraged in a culture of this type, it does not occur to the tradition-directed character, as Riesman puts it, "that he might shape his own destiny in terms of personal, lifelong goals or that the destiny of his children might be separate from that of the family group."

This does not mean that the individuals in such a society are necessarily happy or psychically more stable than those in other societies. But the urge to change which personal unrest elsewhere brings is here braked down by ritual, routine, and the "power relations" among various age and sex groups—clans, castes, professions, and so on.

This society is by no means restricted to the European Middle Ages, but can be found also, as Riesman indicates, among the Hindus or the Hopi Indians, the Zulus or the Chinese, North African Arabs or the Balinese. It is what is frequently characterized as "folk society" as against "civilization," or "status society" as against "contract society," *Gemeinschaft* as against *Gesellschaft*. In general, it puts its premium on external conformity.

By contrast with the tradition-directed character, the inner-directed character is one whose objectives and patterns of activity are dominated by a desire to "make something of himself." "Societies in which inner-direction becomes important, though they are concerned with behavioral conformity, cannot be satisfied with behavioral conformity alone." In the face of novel situations, the problem of personal choice becomes paramount. In the tradition-directed society, choice is channeled through rigid social organization. In the society of the inner-directed, choice is channeled through highly individualized character.

In Western history, the inner-directed character comes to the fore as a typical product at the time of the Renaissance. This is the age of the agonizing examination of conscience, the age of interior searching, Catholic and Protestant as well. Moral theology becomes a well developed discipline; cases of conscience are gone into exhaustively; the *Spiritual Exercises* are drawn up by St. Ignatius Loyola, generated in the very process of his discovering what he was going to make of himself; the notion of "vocation," religious and secular, comes to the fore; and the Protestant ethic matures, sanctifying "hard work" and achievement.

Renaissance inner-directedness was not entirely new. In particular, some of the roots of the Protestant ethic have been traced by Max Weber and others to medieval monasticism, which is in many ways a phenomenon characteristic of tradition-directed society but which, with its goal of self-perfection, carries in itself the germ of inner-directedness, of a drive toward activity which comes primarily from within. Thus the nineteenth century self-made man, burning with "enterprise" and with the conviction that what is good for him must somehow make for progress and be good for the rest of the world, appears as a kind of secularization of the monk, burning with interest in his own interior life.

In comparison with the character produced by Renaissance and post-Renaissance Western society, Catholic and Protestant, the tradition-directed character seems curiously indolent or lazy. Of course, the man of such a character is indolent only by inner-directed standards. He is quite willing to do hard things, many of them too hard for most inner-directed persons. The early American Indian could steel himself to suffering which crushed Europeans. But, as a tradition-directed character, he did not know the inner compulsion to work. The tradition-directed man has simply not been conditioned to feel that one must drive toward distant generalized goals not actually defined by simple conformity to traditional patterns and actions. He is trained to set a premium on fitting into a fixed pattern, not on changing himself or anything else. And, as many a crusader for Western inner-directedness will ruefully acknowledge, it is not easy to "prove" to such a character that he gains anything by developing "drive," by becoming more inner-directed. The very suppositions back of any attempted proof are to him dull and uninteresting.

Finally, the other-directed character is one which arises as a reaction to inner-directedness. Riesman regards this other-directed character as still emergent, not as a type fully developed anywhere in the world. This character receives its motivation not from a whole tradition assimilated en bloc, but from a calculated study of other individuals as individuals, from observing, more or less deliberately, what others are here and now doing, in order to set bearing by their performance and by their reaction to one's own performance. If the nineteenth and twentieth century robber baron of the business world was a typical inner-directed character, powered by his own personal convictions and apologizing to no one, the present-day American junior business executive is the typical other-directed type. Operating in a network of surveys whereby he constantly adjusts and readjusts himself, he is openly self-conscious not only about his business success but even about what others think of his calling, about his business as a personal activity. This type of character, Riesman finds, is "friendlier, more uncertain of himself and his values, more demanding of approval" than is the inner-directed type.

These concepts of tradition-directedness, inner-directedness, and other-directedness admit of indefinite elaboration, and one way to elaborate them is to apply them to concrete situations. If we do this, following Riesman's suggestion that the American character tends more than other characters to the other-directed type, it should be fairly clear that some of the more obvious aspects of American

Catholicism can be explained by the fact that it is other-directed by comparison with French Catholicism. In the first place, it exists in a society which, by comparison with European society in general, is other-directed. Gallup polls, advertisers' surveys, the relatively open, nontheoretical nature of American political parties, the human-interest (that is, reader-interest) approach so deeply rooted in American journalism, the advanced state of popular culture media such as the comics and movies, the social emphasis in the educational program (by contrast, European schools appear to Americans rather as brain factories where isolated individuals are formed on intellectual assembly lines)—all these, and other similar phenomena, are evidence of the American's way of keeping "feelers" out among his fellow men and measuring himself by them. Inevitably, American Catholicism shapes itself to this American world—after all, the Church's Catholicity fits her to redeem society in all its forms.

The American Catholic parish is far more "open" from every point of view than most European parishes. The parishioners are far more conscious of one another, no matter what their economic status. This fact is a correlative of the fact that the American Catholic family is more open than its European counterpart. The subtitle "a magazine for the open family" (*la famille ouverte*) used by the excellent lay-directed Catholic family review of spirituality, *Foyers,* would not have the relevance in America which it does in France, where the closer-knit, more self-conscious family organization is at once a blessing and a handicap. Similarly, the work of the American priest in certain of its aspects is regularly formulated in terms of "service" to the faithful. This focus on service, referred to in the foregoing chapter, is nothing really new, in a way, when we recall such old expressions as *servus servorum Dei,* and yet it is new in its emphasis in so far as the shift from serv*ants* to serv*ice* moves out of the age of feudalism into the age of filling stations, which render service by *studying* what large numbers of transient individuals want. The old-time servant was supposed to know instinctively or by a training which formed his *inner* character, whereas the filling-station attendant learns what is wanted of him rather by study which is analytic and dispassionate, and which thus, in principle, leaves no mark on his person and tends not to place him in any socially inferior position. This is not to say that the present emphasis in the other-directed society can be written off as simply depersonalizing, for the field of personality is complex and cluttered with paradox, so that in many ways this emphasis can represent a more studious attention to the wants of others than ever before.

IV

By contrast with American Catholicism, European Catholicism is commonly thought of as more "traditional." And yet, there are curious paradoxes here which throw light not only on European but also on American Catholicism; for almost all the avowed efforts to adjust the Church positively to the modern world, from the more avant-garde theological speculation through revision of the liturgy and social experiments such as that of the priest-workers and *Mitbestimmungsrecht,* are initiated typically in Europe, not in the United States. Demographic surveys of Catholic practice in Mass attendance are easier to come by in France or Belgium than in the United States, for the Church in France or Belgium wants more to be conscious of her adjustments or failures. On the other hand, the myriad adjustments of American Catholics to the changing world have characteristically been made unconsciously, often with the aid of heavy disguises and all sorts of rationalization. The Church's assimilation of American "optimism," of coeducation, of the world of sports, of the world of commerce—taboo for the most part to the medieval Church—these and many other such things mentioned elsewhere in the present work have been absorbed into the Church in America under a steady barrage of protest from within the Catholic mind itself and without the aid of much theory to justify their absorption. (There still is practically no theory of these things in American Catholic theology.)

It appears that the American Catholic was adjusted to these

things simply by the other-directedness which he picked up from his American heritage—and picked up quickly, for many, if not most, of the Catholic immigrants came from cultures where the Catholic character tended to be a tradition-directed rather than an inner-directed one. Because the other-directed character, in so far as he is other-directed, characteristically receives his motivation from others, the process of adaptation involves practically no violent interior *re*orientation. His other-directedness is his guarantee of stability, since it keeps him interiorly responsive to changes in the world about him. The protests against adaptation were relicts of Old World attitudes, and doomed to die out. Even with their dying out, the other-directed character has produced no mature theory of Catholic adaptation to America. The adaptation is so much taken for granted that no one seems to think that there is anything to explain about it.

For the inner-directed Frenchman, on the other hand, adjustment to environment entails a conscious interior reorientation. Like the American, the modern European, and in particular the modern Frenchman, is quite willing to break with tradition. In France the *notion* of the Revolution has certainly won: practically everybody is "Left," at least in his own estimation, even the blackest reactionary. It is a social outrage to be anything else, and from this point of view it is a mistake to try to think of the French Catholic as typically more "traditional" than the American. But his way of being nontraditional is different: the Frenchman is not tradition-directed because he is inner-directed, whereas the American is not tradition-directed because he is other-directed. The Frenchman is the *self*-conscious revolutionary—he wants to dedicate himself to change in an aggressive fashion in order to achieve a new personal integrity. The American holds his integrity from the beginning in terms of change, and to him all dedication to revolution seems highly pretentious and entirely superfluous.

Helping to account for the high intellectual charge of French Catholicism is its inner-directed character. Intellectuals tend to be inner-directed folk. This is true even in America, and it is not surprising that at its high intellectual levels American Catholicism tends to have great sympathy for French Catholicism (and for much German Catholicism which has this same inner-directedness). Indeed, American Catholic intellectualism is notoriously reliant on French and other European sources for the intellectual stimuli lacking in its own environment—and thus, to continue the ironic dialectic, to this extent other-directed despite itself. It is typical that the late Père A.-J. Maydieu, O.P., editor of *La Vie intellectuelle*, had to come to the United States recently actually to beg American Catholics to write a book about themselves for Europeans and the rest of the Church.

V

The same inner-directedness is related to the French Catholic's hankering to live in a perpetual state of crisis so uncongenial to the "optimistic" American Catholic. This aspect of the French character is what the Frenchman himself will think of and describe as "seriousness," and what the foreigner is likely to identify with sheer contrariness or contumacy. It can generate that most French of all temptations and vices: *Je-m'en-foutisme*—a to-hell-with-everything attitude which in an American would be mere defeatism, but which in France is somehow intimately related to the production of an endless succession of brilliant plays, novels, paintings, and sculptures, and that not only in the present but to some extent as far back as the Gothic lace of medieval French cathedrals, soaring out of disdain into the empyrean with their burden of ethereal and winsome—and, it must be owned, somewhat supercilious—stone madonnas. This is no climate for the Pollyanna Catholicism which is sometimes said to breed under American skies. It is the climate of artistic *productivité.*

But other kinds of *productivité* must exploit other kinds of forces. And when Frenchmen set about imitating *productivité* of the American factory kind, they are likely to forget this fact and to make the mistake of wanting to throw out of their industrial and commercial world all the "inane American optimism," so as to preserve the proper atmosphere of crisis—oblivious of the fact that what produces a Cézanne or a Péguy is not exactly what produces automobiles.

The intimate relation of production to American optimism is interestingly documented by current linguistic research and can be used further to point up the difference between the American and French sensibility. Dorothy Lee has recently made a study of the development of expressions in America featuring the verbal "up"—as in wash *up*, fix *up*, bundle *up*, write *up*. These formations are a recent and distinctive feature of American speech, and Miss Lee finds in them correlatives of the typical American way of facing the world as a series of successive limit-situations—like units in an assembly line. The American sets up his motivation by conceiving of things in terms of a "defining and stiffening limit." (Washing *up* a car is a more limited or "framed" conceptualization than simply washing a car.) Americans commonly prefer "getting a job" to "getting work," or doing a "job" to doing a "task." A job—French and other foreign languages have had to annex the American word itself to lay hold of the American concept—is something bundled up, packaged, a "limit situation." By means of such conceptualization, the American can face life as a series of successes just about to be accomplished. The resulting atmosphere of achievement both generates and feeds on "optimism."

This limit-situation or job mentality is a natural one for the other-directed character. Operating typically in what sociologists call a "peer group," he habitually views his performance less as a projection of his own self (in the way the inner-directed character might) than as something to be measured against the performance of others at every separate instant, piecemeal. He must constantly verify his contact with the "others," the "outside" from which his compulsions derive.

The other-directed is constantly receiving motivation from the other, whereas the inner-directed character is motivated by its desire to do something with itself, so that relationship with others tends to be highly selective, being controlled in terms of foreseeable effects on the self. Thus, whereas in the United States the other-directed character sends its "feelers" farther and farther out into society, finally coming to the point where, in a certain sense, it reacts to all other individuals as to a peer group, in France, on the other hand, there are only special, limited peer groups in which the typically inner-directed character *elects* to enlist. This means that for Catholics in France there is no Serra Club, bringing together active Catholic laymen from all walks of life—two lawyers, two physicians, two manufacturers, two bankers, and so on—but rather highly "specialized" groups such as the *Union sociale des ingénieurs catholiques* for Catholic engineers and production men, or the *Conférence Laënnec* for Catholic physicians.

In these specialized movements French Catholicism (and European Catholicism generally) has achieved splendid results and promises still greater ones. At the same time this inner-directedness produces its own type of difficulty characteristic of the Church in France as of France herself, and to a certain extent of all Europe. For not only does inner-directedness, the feeling that one is driven from within, often make a crisis of any adaptation, but it creates a situation in which adaptation or adjustment to what is outside one is likely to be defined in terms of one's own interior crises—likely, that is, to be itself a product and a perpetuation of inner-directedness.

VI

This set in the French (and Continental) character helps explain many things which to an American are anomalies, first and foremost the fact that, although the Revolution has so long been over with and won, so that everybody is a Leftist, in a sense it has never really been fought. For dedication to Revolution has become a principle not merely of conservation but of out-and-out reaction. This is, of course, inevitable, for the only successful revolution is the unconscious one, or evolution. To enunciate the principle of revolution as a principle is to demolish it, in so far as it is to base one's program more or less negatively on an analysis of a special set of conditions in society, which already necessarily belong to the past by the time they have been analyzed. Only a radically static, nonhistorical view of reality (a view which is itself a thing of the past) can make convincing a dedication to revolution as revolution. The irony in the French (and Continental European) Catholic intellectual situation is to be found in the curious mixture of consciously cultivated historical sense and subconscious reactionism, inherent in the Continental Revolutionary tradition itself, just as the irony in the American Catholic situation is to be found in the nearly total absence of a conscious historical sense despite the other-directed character's imperturbably practical adjustment to change.

The Revolutionary mentality as an outgrowth of inner-directedness helps explain such things as the Communist vote of great numbers of Frenchmen, even those more or less aware of their Catholic heritage. It is commonplace that, to a large extent, this vote does not express appreciation of the Communist Party's real purposes and sympathy with them, but that most Frenchmen and Frenchwomen who vote this way do so rather as the most spectacular means of expressing personal antagonism toward management. The "owners" are here not the class defined by Marxist theory but simply the "others" to which the self, with all its inner problems, is opposed.

This kind of inner-directed psychology makes a classless society really quite unrealizable, for there must always be this "other" opposed to the self in such a way that the self can attack it. Such a psychology accounts for the European's difficulty in grasping imaginatively what an American-type society is. Breaking through a class system to an American means abandoning the notion of class altogether, or at least making movement between classes so easy and frequent that the borderlines themselves cease to be meaningful. Breaking through a class system for a European is likely to mean breaking out of this particular class into another class just as particular. This has been one of the difficulties connected with the priest-worker experiment, which has been advised in papal documents against unwary acceptance of the doctrine of class struggle. In moving to help the workingman, a European Catholic has difficulty remembering that his objective—however difficult of achievement—is to abolish antagonisms, not merely to abandon one side for another.

Of course, the American Catholic would have exactly the same difficulty as the European were he in the European's place. The United States did not become other-directed by design, or even consciously. And the American Catholic, who, in many if not most cases, as has been suggested earlier, passed directly from a tradition-directed to an other-directed stage, must remember with all humility that he is far less well situated to advise French and other European Catholics about their own problems than he is to profit from their continued achievements. Generally when an American Catholic is overpowered by a desire to give advice, the only kind of advice he has to give is imperceptive and boorish enough: try to be as much like us Americans as possible.

But even apart from such offensive formulas, probably any advice from any quarter will only reenforce France's (and Europe's) inner-directedness, for any *conscious* movement of the inner-directed character even toward other-directedness in a way only defeats its own purpose, since it means trying to become other-directed for inner-directed reasons. To a certain extent, France and French Catholicism are evolving in this fashion today. Indeed, the European situation has called for a program of *calculated* "democratization." This is what has produced such typically European phenomena as Socialist parties. Europe has never wanted advisers, and she may remain for an indefinite period more self-conscious in her moves than the United States.

The differences between European and American Catholicism must be faced with a clear acknowledgment that there is no simple moral discrimination possible between the inner-directed and the other-directed character, and that the two, indeed, represent not absolute distinctions but merely different emphases. Each can learn indefinitely from the other, so that the only plan of action, inside the Church and outside, is to encourage friendly contact and understanding—which means to be willing to change ourselves, not others, when we learn how to do so for the better.

4

THE RENAISSANCE MYTH AND THE AMERICAN CATHOLIC MIND

THE EXPERIENCE OF the Renaissance era is deeply imbedded in the American psyche. The Americas were discovered by men of the Renaissance and colonized by them. The very political units into which the Americas are broken down are often the products not of indigenous political and geographical experience but of Renaissance and post-Renaissance man's skill at cartography. Alexander VI's imaginary straight line separating the domains of Spain and Portugal no longer exists, but the map still registers the total abstractions called Colorado and Wyoming in their impudent quadrangularity, their boundaries disdainful of all topographical reality.

Even more than upon the surface of the earth, the Renaissance era has imposed itself upon the American mind. The great religious division of the peoples of the Americas is a Renaissance division, that into Catholic and Protestant. (There is, of course, the smaller, related complement of Jews.) This division cuts across national boundaries and transcends racial groups, and it is not tempered or complicated, as in the Old World, by association with pre-Renaissance religious groupings, such as Islam or Buddhism or Confucianism. In a very real sense—although of course not in every sense—it is true that the American approach to the world, material and religious, begins with the age of the Renaissance.

The Renaissance heritage weighs particularly heavily upon the consciousness of the Catholic in the United States, helping to fix there the nostalgic medievalism which is a hallmark of the Catholicism of English-speaking America and particularly of the United States, and to determine American Catholic attitudes toward history. (I use "American" hereafter to refer specifically to the United States unless a special context clearly indicates a wider meaning for the term.) The American Catholic has been taught by the Renaissance to place some sort of premium upon a revival of the past, although, like other religiously minded persons, he seeks not a revival of pagan antiquity but of a religious Golden Age. His Golden Age is not the same as that of the old-line Protestant, for whom the Golden Age to be recovered by his "reformation" was a reputedly "simple" and hypothetically "pure" Christianity situated in the early Christian era. For the Catholic any such Golden Age is without meaning doctrinally; nevertheless, the American Catholic tends to find something like a Golden Age in medieval times, which he imagines as 100 per cent Catholic (and 100 per cent European, too). The pull of this sort of medievalism can be seen in the personnel, the curriculums, and the publications of Catholic faculties of theology and philosophy, not to mention literature, throughout the country. There are many individuals who must be excepted, but as a whole the Catholic intellectual effort in America remains medieval in focus and intent by comparison not only with the Protestant American effort but by comparison also with the efforts of Catholics in European countries.

This medievalism involves curious states of tension, in which, for example, the Renaissance nostalgia for antiquity, still present in the remnants of classical humanism possessed by American Catholics, is made to defeat itself by feeding the desire for a return to what the Renaissance disowned—the centuries which immediately preceded it. American Catholic educational objectives particularly suffer from unnecessary complications and difficulties by reason of the confusions here. Some of the difficulties have been excellently documented, and in part prescribed for, by Father George E. Ganss in his recent book *St. Ignatius' Idea of a Jesuit University*. The present treatment does not undertake to recommend any particular cures, but it does undertake a re-examination of the Renaissance and the medieval question with particular reference to facts and considerations bearing on current American Catholic attitudes. Re-examination of the myth here must be a prelude to any prescriptions which others, better qualified than I, may perhaps see fit to make.

II

In treating of humanism in letters during the Renaissance and its relevance to American Catholicism, perhaps at the very beginning I should make it clear that I place little stock in Renaissances or renascences as expressive of cultural objectives. For two reasons. First, we have no warrant for attempting to revive the past. Indeed, we have not even the possibility of reviving it. The past, if it is anywhere at all, is in us. Outside the present, there is no past. As Gertrude Stein once remarked, there is one thing everybody is, and that is contemporary. We can, of course, understand ourselves better by studying the past which made us, and which is in us. Indeed, there is no substitute for this kind of study. With it, culture is possible. Without it, there is only a void. But such study is not a Renaissance.

The second reason that I put little stock in renascences is that they imply a cyclic view of history seemingly contrary to the Christian historical sense, which is developmental and evolutional. Besides, the more we learn about evolution, cosmic and phylogenetic, the less ground there seems to be from the point of view of natural science for a cyclic view of history. There may be swirls and eddies in history, but the process as a whole has linear direction: it does not move in circles, as the pagans used to think it did. Not only individuals, but species, evolve and die, never to appear again. The age of the dinosaur is behind us, apparently, for good. Extinct species do not, so far as we know, ever re-form themselves.

There is, indeed, one renascence for each man, baptism, when he is born again in Christ, but this only sets him firmly in his particular place in the forward-moving swing of creation and redemption, which has for each man a beginning and an end. There is, of course, another renascence, the renascence of the seasons, but this has been assimilated into the Church's liturgical year, which as a commemoration moves in a cycle, but commemorates events which do not move in a cycle at all, but are fixed points in the trajectory described by history: the life, death, and resurrection of Christ. These occurred only once, although they are with us always.

But the notion of the Renaissance is with us, too, and we cannot do away with the term. It represents the way we have learned to describe and to think of the period between the Middle Ages and the modern world. The description is in great part a product of our state of mind; but our state of mind is itself an inheritance from the Renaissance age, which conceived of itself, if at first somewhat tentatively and sporadically, still deliberately and consistently, as a rebirth of an older culture.[1] One of the strangest things about the Renaissance, and one of the things which gives it its curiously artificial air, is this fact that it dictates the formula which later ages are to apply to it. The age of classical antiquity does not think of itself as either antiquity or as classical. The Middle Ages have no idea that they are particularly the middle of anything. Only the Renaissance, when it arrives, knows very well what it is. The vision of Petrarch on the mountain in Vaucluse is, indeed, ambiguous, not the clear prophecy of a restored antiquity which Jacob Burckhardt made it out to be. But by Poggio's and certainly by Erasmus' day, the men who were after the classical manuscripts and in the excavations were quite sure that their age is that marked by a renaissance of an ancient culture once dead; they began the first cautious attempts to establish the term "Renaissance" itself.[2]

It is disconcerting and annoying to have an age announce to future ages the terms on which it itself is to be understood and inter-

[1] See Wallace K. Ferguson, *The Renaissance in Historical Thought: Five Centuries of Interpretation* (Boston: Houghton Mifflin Company, 1948).

[2] Ferguson, *op. cit.*, pp. 8, 19, 65, notes that Boccaccio speaks of a restoration of letters, and that the term *la rinascita* was applied without further specification to the beginnings of the (Italian) Renaissance by Giorgio Vasari (b. 1511).

preted. Little wonder that the past generation or two of scholars have thrown themselves into the task of proving that, in one way or another, the Renaissance was not really a Renaissance at all, or was preceded by so many other renaissances—the Carolingian renaissance, the renaissance of the twelfth century, the renaissance of the thirteenth century—as to be, in the last analysis, quite undistinguished. Still, in the dialogue which is recorded history, although one can controvert what has been said, one can never write it completely off the record. The notions one objects to infect one's own mind. The notion of the Renaissance has been extraordinarily infectious, particularly in Catholic circles today, where it is applied to all sorts of things expressive of cultural objectives. This is doubtless because it favors a doubling-back or recuperative movement in the approach to history which, at least at first blush, is congenial to the conservative instincts of Catholics, who, quite understandably, like to maintain their hold on the past.

To these instincts (Catholics have, or should have, other instincts, too), the Renaissance and its humanism undoubtedly recommends itself not only on the intrinsic grounds of its advocacy of a liberal education, but also because it is itself a conservative or recuperative movement. The return to classical humanism recovers simultaneously two points in the past: the postmedieval world and the classical world it purportedly enfolds.

But, while the study of history can bring wisdom by helping us better to understand persistent issues, there is no point of return in human history after the Fall where the issues with which we are interested in dealing were really resolved. The embarrassment which this fact brings to all return movements can be examined on the American Catholic scene, where at present we find side by side, and often in the same persons, an advocacy of humanism envisioned more or less in a Renaissance framework if only because it was the Renaissance which gave the term currency, and an advocacy of a return to the scholasticism of the Middle Ages.

The present essay attempts to deal with some of the relationships and conflicts between these two points of return, Renaissance humanism and medieval scholasticism, not covering the question from all possible points of view, but specializing somewhat in recent discoveries about these two cultural epochs as these affect the American Catholic outlook. Because they are recent, made by our own age in terms of our own interests, these discoveries will perhaps clarify our own insights and refine our concepts of humanism and scholasticism so that we can better think through the issues with which they, and we, are involved.

III

It is very difficult to reconcile any all-out approval of medieval scholasticism with an all-out approval of Renaissance humanism. The two are polar opposites, so much so that, although the degree of resistance varied from individual to individual, a Renaissance humanist habitually defined himself by opposition to scholastic philosophy. We know what St. Thomas More thought of the most taught and undoubtedly the best known of all works by scholastic philosophers, the *Summulae logicales* of the contemporary of St. Thomas Aquinas in thirteenth century Paris, Peter of Spain. With a scorn which he could count on other humanists to share, in speaking of the most original part of this work, the collection of treatises on the properties of terms called the *Parva logicalia* or *Little Logicals,* More refers to it as

> that impossible book (*liber ille*), the *Little Logicals,* which I suppose is so named because it contains so little logic, with its suppositions, as they are called, its ampliations, restrictions, and appellations, wherein it presents picayunish rules which are not only clumsy but even wrong, as when they set themselves to distinguish enunciations of this sort, "Leo animali est fortior" and "Leo est fortior animali," as though they both did not mean the same thing.[3]

[3] Sir Thomas More, Letter to Martin Dorp, from Bruges, October 21 (1515), in *The Correspondence of Sir Thomas More,* ed. by Elizabeth Frances Rogers (Princeton: Princeton University Press, 1947), pp. 38–39. My translation from the Latin.

Perhaps the reason why we can today with a certain equanimity idealize at the same time Renaissance humanism and medieval scholastic philosophy is that we know so little directly of medieval scholastic philosophy. This is as true of neoscholastic philosophers today as of any others, for what passes today for scholastic or neoscholastic philosophy, in so far as it derives from medieval sources, derives almost entirely not from scholastic philosophers but from scholastic theologians—which is not at all the same thing—and, to a large extent, from only one scholastic theologian, to be sure the greatest of them all, St. Thomas Aquinas. Yet there was a real scholastic philosophy which was not at all theology, and there were scholastics who were not at all theologians—thousands of them, indeed, most of them—for besides the arts professors or masters of arts, who alone included the teaching of philosophy among their prerogatives of office and who at Paris excluded St. Thomas and all members of religious orders from their number, there were also the lawyers and doctors of medicine, who were quite as scholastic in their way as the theologians were in theirs.

At Paris, teaching masters of arts, who as such had studied not one iota of theology and who were not necessarily priests or students for the priesthood at all, commonly outnumbered teaching doctors of theology ten to one.[4] There would be even fewer theologians at other universities, for Paris was the theological capital of the world.

Today, practically none of these scholastic philosophers is known in neoscholastic circles. The works of the great figures among them, William of Ockham, Walter Burleigh, Albert of Saxony, Ralph Strode, who was Chaucer's friend and dedicatee, and all the rest, have never even been edited for some four hundred years, so that, even if one wanted to, it is all but impossible to read them on any scale anywhere in the United States. Peter of Spain's *Summulae logicales,* which gave its name to the first-year philosophy students,

[4] See Hastings Rashdall, *The Universities of Europe in the Middle Ages,* newly edited by F. M. Powicke and A. B. Emden (Oxford: Clarendon Press, 1946), III, 331–38. Cf. the lists for the year 1362 and other years in Henri-Suso Denifle and E. Châtelain (eds.), *Chartularium Universitatis Parisiensis* (Paris, 1889–1897), Vols. I and II, *passim.*

called *summulistae*, at the University of Paris for some two hundred years,[5] and which ran through at least 160 editions between the invention of printing and 1530, abruptly thereafter practically ceased to be heard of,[6] remaining unedited in modern times until 1947. Its author, a hundred times more read than his contemporary St. Thomas and famous also as a doctor of medicine, is almost unknown even by name in neoscholastic circles. Yet in the statutes of the arts faculty, to which professors of philosophy belonged, Peter of Spain is the one author of the high Middle Ages who merits a place beside Aristotle, and who is commented on indifferently, like Aristotle, by nominalists and realists, Scotists and Thomists, alike.

It is Peter of Spain who is the favorite target of the Renaissance humanists: he is one of the leading *barbari* with Buridan, Dullaert, and Tartaret, says Peter Ramus;[7] in fact, the ultimate barbarian in dialectic, says Johann Caesarius.[8] Rudolph Agricola, from whom so much in Renaissance dialectic or logic stems, wrote his *Dialectical Invention,* many persons thought, simply to be different from Peter of Spain.[9] The scholastic philosophers or arts-course scholastics

[5] Peter Ramus says that in his day at Paris students in the first three years of philosophy were called respectively *summulistae, logici,* and *physici,* and those in the remaining one-half year *intrantes* (those entering on their career as teachers —a concept surviving in our term "commencement")—Ramus, *Proöemium reformandae Parisiensis Academiae,* in his *Scholae in liberales artes* (1569), col. 1075. For earlier use of *summulistae* and *logici* in this sense, see the 1464 decree of Louis XI for the College of Navarre in Jean de Launoy, *Regii Navarrae Gymnasii Parisiensis historia* (Paris, 1677), I, 170 (Pars I, Lib. II, cap. ix).

[6] See the count in Joseph P. Mullally, *The "Summulae Logicales" of Peter of Spain* (Indiana: University of Notre Dame Press, Publications in Medieval Studies, 1945), pp. 132–58. This count is based entirely on an examination of printed library catalogues and other printed catalogues available in the United States. There are certainly rather more than these 160 early editions.

[7] Peter Ramus, *Pro philosophica Parisiensis academiae disciplina oratio* (1551), in his *Scholae in liberales artes* (Basle, 1569), col. 1049.

[8] J. Caesarius, *Dialectica* (Lugduni, 1556), p. 191.

[9] Agricola's editor, Johannes Matthaeus Phrissemius, protests vigorously against this opinion, saying that Agricola treats *de effectibus* or emotional appeal because this is really relevant to dialectic and not just because Peter of Spain did not treat it. See Phrissemius' "Argumentum operis" in Rudolph Agricola, *De inventione dialectica libri tres, cum scholiis Ioannis Matthaei Phrissemii* (Paris, 1529), copy in the Bibliothèque Nationale, Paris. Whether or not Agricola did so designedly, he certainly succeeded in differing with Peter of Spain, and that was what counted.

headed by Peter of Spain are the typical scholastics who bear the brunt of the attack by the humanists, many of whom, like More or Erasmus, will go out of their way on occasion to defend the theologian Aquinas, dissociating him from scholastic philosophy and putting him with the Fathers of the Church.[10]

IV

In the face of these anomalies, it is obvious that our way of thinking about medieval scholasticism, the Renaissance, and the whole complex of relationships involved in the periods covered by these terms, needs re-examination. We live in an age which associates philosophy, including what we take to be the continuation of scholastic philosophy, with such subjects as literature and history, and sets the whole somewhat apart from science. We are inclined to impute a similar alignment to the Middle Ages and the Renaissance. Present-day studies make it daily increasingly clear that in both the Middle Ages and much of the Renaissance, philosophy as such was aligned with the physical sciences and thus set against literary studies.

In terms of this alignment, the rediscovery of the scholastic philosophers at present under way is a phenomenon interesting in the extreme because of the quarters from which it proceeds. It is the result of two currents of interest, the one represented in the nineteenth and early twentieth century chiefly by Pierre Duhem, and in our own time by Lynn Thorndike, John Herman Randall, Jr., Herbert Butterfield, Anneliese Maier, A. C. Crombie, and an increasing number of others interested in the history of scientific thinking; and the other represented by Jan Lukasiewicz, the late Father Philotheus Boehner, O.F.M.; Ernest A. Moody, Father Joseph T. Clark, S.J.; Willard Van Orman Quine, Father I. M. Bochenski, O.P.; and others trained in the tradition of modern symbolic or mathematical logic developed by Frege, Boole, White-

[10] See Edward L. Surtz, S.J., "'Oxford Reformers' and Scholasticism," *Studies in Philology,* XLVII (1950), 547–56.

head, Carnap, and others. This renewed interest in medieval scholastic philosophy—as against medieval scholastic theology and its philosophical derivatives—has thus been the result of neoscholastic effort hardly at all. Scholastic philosophy has proved interesting to physicists and formal logicians.

This fact is one of the best indexes we could have of the nature of medieval scholastic philosophy as a whole. For logic and physics was what scholastic philosophy during the Middle Ages in great part consisted in. We have only to look at university arts faculty statutes to see this.[11] If our own reluctance to own the neglect of metaphysics in the philosophy course is not overcome by the evidence in these statutes, or by the fact that the medieval student finished *all* philosophy normally around the age of eighteen or twenty[12] (whereupon he was immediately qualified to teach all philosophy), or by the fact that the scholastic metaphysics known today is never that of medieval scholastic philosophers but that extracted from medieval theologians, it will perhaps be given a rude shock by the letter which the philosophy faculty at Paris, the world capital of medieval scholasticism, addresses to the Dominican chapter at Lyons on the occasion of the death of Frater Thomas Aquinas, requesting certain books which he had had in progress shortly before his death and of which they are extremely anxious to secure copies. Of the *Summa theologiae,* the arsenal of neoscholastic metaphysics and the work which everyone thinks of when St. Thomas's unfinished works are mentioned today, the letter says not one word. This was a *theological* document, and the present letter is from the arts faculty, the faculty of grammar, rhetoric, and scholastic *philosophy.*

The projected works of Frater Thomas mentioned in this letter are (1) a commentary on an unidentified work of the Neo-Platonist Simplicius (whose studies of Aristotle's treatise *The Heavens* and of Aristotle's *Physics* were well known, and who was so thoroughly identified with questions of celestial geography as to give his name

[11] See the statutes in the *Chartularium Universitatis Parisiensis* for the years 1215, 1252, 1255, 1366, and 1452. Cf. Rashdall, *op. cit.,* I, 439–50.

[12] Rashdall, *ibid.,* I, 247, 303, 462, 472, 474, and references there.

to one of the interlocutors in Galileo's famous *Dialogue on the Two World Systems*); (2) a commentary on Aristotle's work itself, *The Heavens and the Earth;* (3) another commentary on Plato's cosmological dialogue, the *Timaeus;* (4) and finally, a book *On How to Put Up Aqueducts and How to Make Mechanical Devices for Military Operations.*[13] Whether Frater Thomas ever got around to finishing these works or even to starting them is inconsequential. The point here is that they were the sort of things that the greatest faculty of scholastic philosophy at the height of the scholastic age was interested in. They make it clear how far gone scholastic philosophy was, and always had been, in the direction of what we should call physical science—rather bad physical science, it turned out, but cultivated with the physical scientists' interests none the less. These men wanted to know what made things in the world go. For, if it is true, as it is, that medieval physics is permeated with metaphysics, it is also true that medieval metaphysics itself was permeated with the physical sciences, where it was not actually smothered by them. The treatises on the soul, for example, are quite different from neoscholastic treatises on the soul today, being commonly full of material on the systole and diastole of the heart, the movements of the supposed "animal spirits," and other matters belonging to physiology and anatomy. It is now known that even the apparently more metaphysical speculation was often serving obscure but important ends in the physical sciences, reorienting the whole mind in ways which would make Newtonian and post-Newtonian physics possible.[14]

Recent discoveries concerning the role of scholastic physics in the complex evolution of thought which has produced the modern physical sciences have been complemented, more recently, by parallel discoveries in scholastic logic. As has already been mentioned, the impetus for rediscovering this logic has come from the modern

[13] *Chartularium Universitatis Parisiensis,* I, 504–5 (No. 447); the letter is dated from Paris, May 2, 1274.

[14] See A. C. Crombie, *Augustine to Galileo: The History of Science, A.D. 400–1650* (London: Falcon Press, 1952); Herbert Butterfield, *The Origins of Modern Science, 1300–1800* (London: G. Bell and Sons, Ltd., 1949); etc.

mathematical logicians in the tradition of Frege, Boole, Whitehead, Lukasiewicz, and their associates. The logic of this tradition has matured under the tutelage of modern mathematico-physical science, of which it forms a kind of abstract complement or structural counterpart. Seeing that the medieval scholastic philosophers have thus proved fascinating from the point of view both of modern physical science and of the formal logic that goes with it, and that medieval scholastic philosophy itself in so great part consisted in logic and physics, one is inclined to suspect that the historical significance of medieval arts scholasticism as a whole may perhaps be more a matter of its relationship to modern mathematico-physical science than to the scholastic philosophy today distilled out of the theology of a St. Thomas, who is quite outside the principal logical current of the Middle Ages. The diversity in outlook which the label "scholastic" actually covers has become commonplace knowledge, particularly since the work of Professor Gilson.

If this is true, and I believe there can no longer be any doubt that it is, then arts scholasticism—which, we cannot remind ourselves too often, was most medieval scholasticism—is to be regarded as radically a forerunner of the scientific world of modern times, as a psychological phenomenon producing in the mind the same temper in many ways (not, of course, in all) as that of the mind today trained in the physical sciences. The affinity between the medieval scholastic mind and the modern scientific mind has, in a general way, been noted frequently enough. But at present the affinity is becoming more significant and detailed. Studies by Boehner and others,[15] as well as other important evidence,[16] show that scholastic logic, highly quantified and reducing readily to symbolic expression, is, in many ways, a kind of pre-mathematics, as *Ur-*

[15] Philotheus Boehner, O.F.M., *Medieval Logic: An Outline of Its Development from 1250 to c. 1400* (Manchester: Manchester University Press, 1952). Ernest A. Moody, *Truth and Consequence in Medieval Logic* (Amsterdam: North-Holland Publishing Co., 1953); this work appears in the series "Studies in Logic and the Foundations of Mathematics," ed. by L. E. J. Brouwer, E. W. Beth, and A. Heyting.

[16] Much of this evidence is adduced in a work which I hope soon to have published, Ramus, Method, and the Decay of Dialogue.

Mathematik. The preparation for the approach to physical science through variables which could be mathematically manipulated—the approach which made possible first Newtonian and then modern field physics—seems to have been made, rather unwittingly to be sure, not only by the impetus theory in scholastic physics but also by supposition theory and related techniques for handling terms developed for the first time in medieval scholastic logic.

This description of arts scholasticism in one of its important aspects has been cast in twentieth century terms and would have been incomprehensible to the medieval or Renaissance mind coming upon it unprepared. But it conveys to us, in our own perspectives, something of the impression which scholastic philosophy made on Renaissance humanists. The philosophy meant a highly specialized education of a scientific sort. The curious fact that this scientism was also controlled by being oriented to teaching because the universities, institutions administered by or for the sake of teachers' unions, were technically normal schools and nothing else, is important, but too vast a matter to be elaborated here. One way or another, scholastic philosophy was identified with a too technical approach to knowledge. The humanists' complaints against the dialectic or logic which governed the arts scholastic program are strikingly like those which an advocate of humanistic education today might make against a purely scientific education: it fills the student with nothing better than technicalities; it is "thorny" or "prickly," arid, dry, and inhuman; or, as Ramus summed it up, does not prepare for life.[17]

V

The past few decades have shown a growing awareness that the Renaissance was, in many of its aspects, antiscientific, and that, far from bringing enlightenment after a period of scholastic darkness, in many ways the humanists succeeded only in turning back

[17] Peter Ramus, *Aristotelicae animadversiones* (Paris, 1543), fols. 67, 77–79—copy in Harvard University Library.

the clock of scientific progress—fortunately, not for long, for there were more than simply humanist forces at work in the Renaissance age. This age was more than a mere reaction against scholasticism —Leonardo da Vinci, for example, represented a protraction of medieval scientific interests and some advance beyond them, as well as their amalgamation with new Renaissance humanistic ideals —but in the field of letters the program of Renaissance humanism was to a great extent defined by its opposition to the ideals and practice of arts scholasticism. Humanists stood for a linguistically rather than a philosophically and scientifically centered training. Lorenzo Valla took the position that, since human cognition is inextricably involved with communication, being cast in terms which are formed so as to be inextricable from language and thus are designed not simply for possessing knowledge but for sharing it with others, all cognition is necessarily bound up with linguistic analysis and must be approached through linguistic.[18]

This sounds something like a recommendation for logic, but it differs from the central logical tradition in its bias against the technicalities necessary for scientizing. Humanists, and even post-Renaissance scholastics more or less under the humanist spell, failed to develop any tools of linguistic analysis equal in keenness to those of medieval logic, however limited and specialized these may have been. Humanist linguistics remained basically rhetorical and historical, an approach to existent texts like that of St. Jerome to the Bible or that of the nineteenth century editors to the classics. It never evolved a mature and viable semantics, preferring philology instead. Language for the humanist was to be used, not too much dismembered. For an Erasmus, education was to be centered on training students to use what appeared to the humanists to be the three great languages of mankind—Latin, Greek, and Hebrew. Textual editing remained paramount in determining linguistic outlooks. Semantics, like logic, was no help in editing St. Paul. One was

[18] See P. Albert Duhamel, "The Oxford Lectures of John Colet," *Journal of the History of Ideas,* XIV (1953), pp. 503–4 and references there.

fitted to do this only when one had mastered Greek so that one could use it and write books in it oneself.[19]

Such linguistically focused educational ideals led Erasmus and other humanists not only to slight dialectic or logic by making it a mere propaedeutic to rhetoric but also proportionately to slight physical science as well, for this tended to be regarded as a mere auxiliary to skill in language. In Erasmus and other humanists, physics simply dies of neglect. Peter Ramus was actually to try to knock the science out of linguistic study altogether, proposing his commentaries on Virgil's *Bucolics* and *Georgics* as a kind of new humanist physics—all that a boy need know of the subject.

VI

To a great extent, in its skimping of medieval quantified logic and physics, the linguistic program of the humanists was what it pretended to be, a return to antiquity, for both the Roman ideal of education and even the normal Grecian ideal [20] had been the formation of a man skilled in the use of words, a rhetorician rather than a philosopher or scientist. But the story of Renaissance ambitions and their fulfillment is a complicated one. For, as a matter of fact, the return to antiquity was a project undertaken by postmedieval men, and the realization of the project is a curious mixture of the ancient and the medieval, the whole controlled by the fifteenth and sixteenth century actuality.

The approach of the Renaissance humanists to language and letters differed from that of the ancients in great part as sight differs from sound. The Renaissance in letters had come into being not within an economy of the spoken word but with the discovery of the written word in the form of classical manuscripts by the generation

[19] Erasmus, *Opus epistolarum*, ed. P. S. Allen (Oxford: Clarendon Press, 1906), I, 404–5.

[20] The fact that it was the oratorical ideal of the Sophists and not the philosophical ideal of Socrates, Plato, and Aristotle which typified the Greek ideal of education and civilization has been made abundantly clear in H. I. Marrou, *Histoire de l'éducation dans l'antiquité* (Paris: Éditions du Seuil, 1950), pp. 268 ff.

of Poggio (1380–1459), Niccoli, and Nicholas of Cusa (1401–1464). The age that was ushered in was primarily a reading age, for humanism failed to revolutionize the speaking habits of the West so much as its writing and reading habits. Latin remained the only really spoken language of the intellectual world of the Renaissance just as it had been in medieval times, and, at the popular level, the vernacular languages continued more than ever their vigorous development as spoken media and even began to be written more and more. The humanist program to revitalize Greek and Hebrew as means of oral expression was never even half realized. Only occasionally were orations in Greek carefully committed to memory and, perhaps on the occasion of a royal "progress" or of an academic exercise, were pronounced painstakingly as showpieces by men or boys who were quite capable of extempore Latin oratory by the hour.

Even in Latin, the classicism of the humanists made itself felt far more in written than in spoken expression. One need only compare the printed works of scholars with the jottings from their lectures preserved in schoolboys' manuscripts to see how, as it fell from the lips, expression could fail to show the classical polish which it developed in being committed to writing. The humanists betrayed their bias for writing in any number of ways. They introduced written exercises into school work, where medieval scholasticism, with its normal-school orientation, had known only oral recitations and performances. By their approach to language through the written word, they completely inverted Cicero's role in the history of Latin at the very time they were proposing him as a model to be imitated in all particulars. For one of Cicero's chief functions had been that of an innovator who invented new Latin words without number to render the Hellenic thought which he brought back to Italy from his studies in Greece. The Renaissance transformed him from an innovator and active catalyst into a fixative, by the simple process of concentrating on his speech as written, and hence as indubitably fixed. Thus Cardinal Bembo's Ciceronianism, with its slavish imitation of Cicero's words, phrases, and even thought, is the exact opposite of

Cicero's own Ciceronianism of innovation. The irony of the situation was not always lost on Renaissance humanists, and it gives rise to the various treatises on Ciceronianism, from Erasmus' to Ramus' and Gabriel Harvey's, which try to resolve the antinomy.

From elementary school on, the status of Latin, the most vocal of the three ancient tongues, had radically changed since Cicero's day; it had changed toward diminished vocalization. It was now a language one learned first to read, and only afterward to speak. Despite Erasmus' ambitions, rhetoric, eminently the art of speaking, never became the culminating course in the educational program as it had been in ancient Greece and Rome. It was made more of than it had been in the Middle Ages, but it remained basically the next course in Latin after grammar before one moved on to the sciences, which were hardly the place for effective oratory. The brave recommendations of a More or a Vives or an Ascham to put the boy in a family where Latin was spoken and spoken well might help somewhat to make Latin an auditory acquisition, but such a move was doomed to relatively little success. For families contained, then as now, an unavoidable complement of women, and—save for a few exceptions whom history never fails to record because they are exceptions, such as Margaret More or Queen Elizabeth—women knew no Latin. One could hardly expect an English or German or French mother to coo to her baby in the language of Cicero.

In the ancient world, language had been bound less to writing and thus less to space, but rather to time, for language had there been felt primarily as something uttered, not as something recorded. *Verba volant, scripta manent.* Spoken words, like time itself, fly. Only when speech is no longer an utterance but the series of marks on a spatial field which we call writing can it endure for more than the moment in which it passes over the lips. The ancient world had, indeed, known writing, but as a subordinate art, committed to scribes rather than to the real rhetorician, and oriented toward oral speech in a way writing is not today. For even when one was reading to oneself, one habitually read aloud—a habit which persisted through the Middle Ages. The literary tradition of the ancient world was the rhetorical tradition, and its greatest figures are orators, Isocrates, Demosthenes, Cicero, Quintilian, or at the very least playwrights such as Sophocles and Aeschylus who composed for oral delivery. The historians are relatively minor figures—and, even so, their histories are not what history is today, but a pastiche of speeches attributed to the characters they write about. Poets, as we know, wrote not to be read silently, but to be recited.

Unlike the ancients for whom language flowed with time, the humanists, in binding language to the written record, on the contrary bound language to space. On the one hand, this proves that the humanists were postmedieval men, sharing the bias of the scientific mind, its passion for the fixed and permanent, even to the neglect of the living, its preference for sight rather than sound. On the other hand, the approach to language through space was inevitable among those who turned, as the humanists did, to the past. For again, *verba volant, scripta manent.* The past is never vocal. The present alone has a voice. The past had only a written record.

These two things, a scientific bias and an affection for the permanence of the written record, go together in the scientific mind which scholasticism had so long been forming, so that it is time we asked ourselves how much humanism was really a reaction against scholasticism and how much it was scholasticism merely shifting its focus of interest from the sciences to the literary monuments of antiquity. For, by the fifteenth and early sixteenth centuries, the humanists' devotion to a written as against a spoken linguistic tradition was not the only evidence of a disposition to feel expression as committed to space rather than as moving with time. This was the age of the development of printing from movable type, the supreme effort to fix the word spatially by reducing it to locally maneuverable units, an altogether curious effort which did not involve a real invention at all, since all the items in use—not only ink and presses and paper or its equivalent, but also engraved dies and castings—had been known from antiquity, so that the real puzzle about printing has always been why it did not come into use earlier. This was also the age which generated that rarest of phenomena, a genuinely new heresy, unknown to antiquity, the Bible heresy, the belief that the sole rule of faith was the words committed to writing by inspired authors. The guardianship of truth was being interpreted as the guardianship of the written word.

The slow death which dialogue suffers over the centuries is clearly on its way here. From this age would emerge dictionaries, wherein the spoken word would be governed by the written, first in the classical and then ultimately even in the vernacular languages. Here lie the roots of the various royal academies and of the eighteenth century attempts to legislate in advance and in writing how a man might be allowed to express himself. This tremendous scientizing apparatus will take time to perfect its operations, but they are all present in germ in the Renaissance commitment to the written as against the spoken word. Erasmus' attitude toward language is complex, but when he insists that the knowledge of "almost everything" is to be sought in the Greek authors, who are the sources or "springs" of all science,[21] there is no mistaking the implication that the written word rules all. As this outlook gains adherents, the notion of what knowledge is and of what logic is, is due to undergo a subtle and important change which, among other things, will help determine the evolution from the Aristotelian notion of analysis through the Ramist notion to that of Descartes and Kant.

VII

A revolution cannot cancel out what it revolts against: it must also live off it. As a revolution against arts scholasticism, humanism also perpetuated in its own way the scientism which this scholasticism had made current. Perhaps enough has been said to show this essentially dialectical relationship of continuity and reaction be-

[21] Erasmus, *De ratione studii . . .* (Strasbourg, 1512), fol. Aii^{v}. The same passage appears somewhat revised, but with its tenor unaltered, in Erasmus' *Omnia opera* (Basle, 1540–42), I, 445. Cf. William Harrison Woodward, *Desiderius Erasmus Concerning the Aim and Method of Education* (Cambridge: The University Press, 1904), p. 164, where the passage is translated, if rather freely.

tween the scholastic and the humanist set of mind and ideals. But humanism is related by continuity and reaction not only to its antecedents but also to its consequents. In the field of letters, to which we are limiting ourselves here, the outcome of humanism is a riot of irony. Among the most striking of the ironies is the fact that this age, which looked on itself and is characterized today as an age of Renaissance, when ancient letters were, in principle, restored, actually turned out to be, on the contrary, the great age rather of the new vernacular literatures—the age of Shakespeare, Montaigne, Cervantes, and their contemporaries.

Since the nineteenth century campaigns to bestow a history on the vernacular literatures, the Renaissance period has been combed for any and all evidence of enthusiasm for the vernaculars. The Pléiade in France, the Countess of Pembroke's little coterie in England, and all the other nativist movements have been publicized till they are almost all we can think of today when we try to reconstruct for ourselves Renaissance literary objectives. We too easily forget that the linguistic ideals of the humanists—who, after all, are in one way or another responsible for the very notion of the Renaissance—had absolutely nothing to do with the vernaculars at all, and that the great figures of vernacular literature in this period were trained not according to the specifications of nineteenth century literary historians interested in composing dictionaries of national biography but according to those of these same humanists, who scorned vernaculars and sometimes nationalism as well.

If the humanist type of training resulted in great vernacular literature, it did so quite by accident and despite itself. In a famous phrase from his verses in the First Folio, Ben Jonson observes that his friend William Shakespeare knew "small Latine and lesse Greeke." This does not surprise the man in the street today, for he supposes that Shakespeare's principal school training was, naturally, in English. It was not. The schoolboy in Shakespeare's day had neither occasion nor opportunity to study English in school, even if he was Shakespeare. His textbooks were in Latin, even for the study of Latin itself, for, practically speaking, no one ever thought of studying in any other medium. The Greek grammars were written in Latin, and the textbooks for geometry and algebra—what little there was of these—were in Latin, too. The vernaculars were learned simply by speaking them—and even this was ordinarily forbidden to boys at school by the rules which officially prescribed Latin for conversation among the students, even during their recreation. The occasional grammars of the English language, which were never used at school, were likely to be themselves in Latin—so as to benefit those who used them, that is, not schoolboys but foreigners.[22] All the serious books which, presumably, one went to school to prepare oneself to read—books on the physical sciences, on philosophy, on medicine, law, or theology, books on history, on alchemy, on astronomy, and all the rest—were in Latin. Only a much later age would see this tradition of Latin for the school-trained man gradually deteriorate. It was not until 1729, for example, that the first lectures delivered in English were given at a Scottish university.[23]

It is, of course, possible by a kind of extrapolation to think of the Renaissance humanists as formulating generically and for all time certain "principles" of humanistic education and then as applying them to the particular conditions which obtained in the sixteenth and seventeenth centuries. Such principles are perhaps implied by the humanists. But they are seldom, if ever, stated, and, if we wish to make use of them, we shall have first to isolate and formulate them ourselves. For the Renaissance humanists, like educators today, had enough to do meeting the problems of the day without legislating for all time.

It is also possible to think in terms of transfer value in training, whereby habits contracted through study in one field equip us for

[22] For example, P[aul] Gr[eaves] or P. Gr[eenwood]? *Grammatica anglicana, praecipue quatenus a Latina differt, ad unicam P. Rami methodum concinnata* . . . (Cambridge, 1594). Significantly, Ramus' own *Gramere* of the French language, written originally in French under the influence of the Pléiade, was translated immediately into Latin, but his Latin grammar (which went through far more editions than the French grammar) was never translated into French.

[23] Norman Kemp Smith, *The Philosophy of David Hume* (London: Macmillan & Co., 1941), p. 23.

study in another or all others. But it is against all the evidence to think that the Renaissance humanists, such as Rudolph Agricola and Erasmus and More and Colet and Vives, thought for a moment of training students in Latin in order to equip them with skill in the vernaculars. What could be the reason for such curious indirection? And what vernacular would Erasmus be skilled in or even interested in? He had lived under nearly all the flags in Christendom. Vives, tutor of Queen Elizabeth, was a Spaniard, and, as it now appears, one of Jewish descent. It would be interesting to know what sort of English he or Erasmus spoke. There is no record, it seems. For it made no difference. These men were teachers and intellectuals, and for teachers and intellectuals only Latin really mattered.

Any frank assessment of the humanist movement in letters must face the fact that all its permanent achievements which strike us today were unintentional and unexpected, or even unwanted. Erasmus would have been the most surprised man in the world had he been told that the age of the College of the Three Languages (Latin, Greek, and Hebrew) at Louvain would be remembered today as the age when vernacular literatures began to come into their own. He would have been perhaps discouraged to learn that the Latin literature which he dreamed of creating on the classical model would be so stillborn that in all the world there has never been written even a modest history of postmedieval Latin literature, and that medieval texts are now re-edited more than those of the humanists. There are, indeed, histories of classical scholarship, for among the express objectives of humanism one at least has been undoubtedly achieved: that of *Wissenschaft,* which is permanently with us, periodically charting the way to the springs of Helicon, drying them up, and reopening them again. Had Erasmus lived to see the sequel to his ambitions, he could have added still another chapter to his *Praise of Folly.*

And yet, however different its forms from those projected by its originators, the heritage of the Renaissance is with us undoubtedly to stay. The Renaissance was an epoch in our own history and in that of all mankind, which we can no more abrogate than the Renaissance itself could abrogate the Middle Ages. We learn from our past by accepting it—critically, to be sure, but wholly and without stint.

One of our debts to the Renaissance in letters is particularly great, for we owe this Renaissance in large part nothing less than our sense of literature itself, a sense which affects us all the way from our interpretation of the simplest prose to our very understanding of the Bible. For, if the Middle Ages wrote literature, they had little sense of a literary tradition, or at least had little interest in cultivating this sense expressly. Medieval education was formalistic and abstractionist—Latin grammar, a rhetoric which was little more than an advanced course in Latin reading and writing, followed by logic and "philosophy," and, for those who wished, by professional courses in medicine, law, or theology. Such training terminates in the Continental-style university of today, where specialization rules uncontested. Even the great medieval school at Chartres, which John of Salisbury reports on so favorably as a quasi-humanistic center of studies, was distressingly formalistic from our point of view. Medieval higher education was largely, in principle, the training of teachers, and the teacher was, more than we should like to have him today, simply a man who analyzed and explained in abstract terms. The notion of a teacher as one who forms the whole man is rather outside the medieval tradition, which on the one hand did not contest this notion, but on the other simply failed to attend to it. The medieval universities were teachers' unions with their apprentices or near apprentices, the students. In principle, these universities trained only teachers and nothing more, for they trained for the reception of a degree, and a degree was simply admission to the teachers' union.[24]

The Renaissance substituted for these educational ideals of the professional teachers' union the somewhat amateur but broader

[24] This was true even at Bologna and other student-directed universities, where reception of a degree thus involved, in a sense, a kind of demotion(!) from the status of student (employer) to master (employee). See Rashdall, *op. cit.*, I, 195–97, 226–28, 283–86, 293 ff., 461 ff.

ideals of a family and larger social group, for the humanists originally grew up not as denizens of the university world but as hangers-on of noble or wealthy bourgeois families, often commissioned to educate the families' younger members, without any design of making them teachers at all. Erasmus' *De civilitate morum puerilium*, with the other books of manners which succeeded it, represented something quite unthought of in medieval formal education. In this context, the humanists brought enthusiasm for literature as literature into the educational scheme. Hitherto, in the Middle Ages, literature, particularly in its oral forms, had indeed been known and loved—but not in the schools. In the form of vernacular mystery plays or recitatives of various sorts, medieval literature was for the unlettered—although not forbidden to the literate and often composed by them—somwhat as radio and television are today. Classical literature was known to the Middle Ages, too, but it was something one dipped into perhaps to improve one's skill in Latin and then ordinarily grew away from as soon as possible so as to devote oneself to the sciences. With the Renaissance, literature as such became the concern of lettered and mature men. And, although at first no one thought of vernacular literature as meriting the attention of men skilled in Latin—except for drama, the best medieval and Renaissance vernacular literature is commonly written for women—it was inevitable that, when vernacular literature matured, it would receive the mature attention Latin and Greek literature had been getting. In the Renaissance the matrix for a full extrascientific literature was formed, and it was into this matrix that the vernacular was later fitted.

Still, the success of the Renaissance in creating a sense of literature should not be exaggerated. On the whole, in terms of the objectives set by the great humanists, the success was poor. Erasmus had envisioned a universe of scholars like Marsilio Ficino and the others at the Florentine Platonic Academy. But, as a matter of fact, the medieval type of study program in great part persisted well beyond Erasmus' age, and even into the nineteenth century. With the advent of humanism, rhetoric, and literature with it, had indeed grown in importance; but, almost everywhere north of the Alps and in the Iberian peninsula, the arts course still sandwiched rhetoric between elementary grammar on the one hand and, on the other, logic and natural science or physics, with a bit of ethics and some gestures toward mathematics and metaphysics. It is a subject for twentieth century meditation that, until not many generations ago, literature was seldom taught to a boy after he was about fourteen years old—and taught to girls of any age almost never. Literary training in any adult or near-adult sense was mostly a matter of free enterprise.

VIII

Although the Renaissance has much to teach us today, what it has to teach us is not necessarily what we want to learn. Sometimes the things we most want to learn are not learnable, because they are not true. It would be consoling to think, as we perhaps like to think, that Renaissance humanism solved the problem of the relationship of science and letters. Unfortunately, it did not. Renaissance humanism brought men to feel more keenly the claims of letters. This was something, for the formal education of the Middle Ages, like our modern scientific rationalism, had commonly been more obtuse. But the Renaissance did not succeed fully in resolving the relationship of science and letters for itself, much less for all time, if only for the reason that this relationship can never be definitively resolved. It invites not final resolution but, rather, practical decisions which have to be made again and again in the concrete circumstances in which practical decisions are made.

Thus it is understandable that Renaissance notions of humanistic education, as they existed in practice—not perhaps as they existed in the mouth of an exponent such as Erasmus—were equivocal, compromising, alternately enthusiastic and reserved, and, in the end, as a matter of fact largely overcome by the scientizing momentum which feeds out of the Middle Ages into our own century. When literary neoclassicism expires, it does so crushed to death by science: among the last major literary projects of the neo-Latin tradition were the 5,000-line poem of the Polish Jesuit scientist Roger John Boscovich celebrating in 1760 the glories of Copernican astronomy and entitled *The Eclipses of the Sun and the Moon* (*De solis ac lunae defectibus*), and Paolo Lucini's 3,000-line verse rendering of Newton's *Opticks*, published in 1793.[25] These late attempts to resolve the tensions between letters and science in something like Renaissance classical formulas did not succeed. For this sort of letters had no fight left in it. It was dead. The classics lived, but you did not write them any more.

The limitations of Renaissance humanism were due to its failure to take its own past wholly into account, and its consequent failure to see itself for what it really was in connection with its own age and those which were to follow. In particular, it scanted the Middle Ages, and, in doing so, misunderstood itself—misunderstood its own inherent formalism and its strong scientizing momentum which would be obscured at first, but which would finally succeed in immobilizing and killing the Latin language vulgarized and so kept alive through the Middle Ages. Erasmus and his friends failed to realize that by fixing on it as a written language, they had given Latin the kiss not of immortality but of death. For language can live only when its existence is precarious, in close connection with the fugitive, spoken word. However, in a sense, the humanists were not a cause so much as an effect of the changing status of Latin, for their appearance on the scene showed that, despite its apparent vigor as a spoken medium, the vernaculars were secretly destined to take over. The death throes of postclassical Latin literature would take centuries, but they had been initiated with Poggio's discoveries and Erasmus' *Dialogues*.

Nevertheless, our persistent interest in humanism in twentieth

[25] See James R. Naiden, "Newton Demands the Latin Muse," *Symposium*, VI (1952), 111–20. The date 1760 is, of course, significant, for only three years before this, the *Index librorum prohibitorum* had finally dropped from among the books forbidden to Catholics those which taught that the earth went around the sun, theretofore included universally as a class. See the article on Galileo in the *Dictionnaire de théologie catholique*.

century America shows that, whatever the fate of Latin as a vehicle for literary production, the Renaissance experience is not and never will be entirely dead. It will live even when its name is forgotten. For it, too, is our past. By studying it, we learn about ourselves. Let us hope that we learn from it as fully as we can. The danger, it would seem, particularly in American Catholic circles, is that the term "humanism" will throw a spell over us, so that to the period which gave currency to this term expressive of so many of our ideals, we attribute a success in implementing such ideals which effectively disables our own efforts by deflecting our attention from our own real problems and our own achievements.

In terms of the sense of literature which we owe so largely to the Renaissance, our own achievements today, if limited, are real. This is particularly true with relation to the academic program, despite all the weaknesses which our present program beyond a doubt exhibits. When we lament the demands of specialized and technological education in the United States, it is well to remember that in many ways we have one of the least specialized educational systems among the technologically advanced countries. The United States is singular in that here the tradition of the humanist college has actually infiltrated the universities. In Europe a student going up to the university to read mathematics will in all likelihood never study a thing but mathematical subjects. If he wishes to study literature or history or philosophy, he will have to elect to study them the same way, as specialized subjects, pursued alone. Despite the pious persuasions of many American enthusiasts for a "broad, humanistic" university education, this specialization is the rule even at Cambridge and Oxford, where we find C. S. Lewis coolly defending the Oxford "specialization" by name. The practice of spreading the courses in the first two years of university work and even later in order to give the student a broadening contact with several fields is characteristically American university practice.

It is true that the European university course leading to the first university degree is begun a year later, more or less, than the American course and that it takes only three years, so that it corresponds to the sophomore, junior, and senior years, the rough equivalent of our freshman year forming a part not of the university but of the secondary-school program. The European university thus has not killed off the general or humanistic subjects, but has rather relegated them to the secondary school, where, it must be confessed, they are generally studied with an intensity foreign to the American sports-and-social-life tradition. Still, in a cultural complex, much depends not only on what subjects are taught, but also on where they are taught. The presence of a program of general education on a university campus means that the highest educational organ of society is not merely a specializing organ, but also in some measure an integrating organ. This the American university certainly is, in however haphazard a way, not only in the vaguely humanistic orientation of part of its study program, but also in its manifold connections linking it to the commercial, financial, trade-union, journalistic, and religious worlds, and to countless other worlds as well, in a way quite strange to European universities.

This distinctively American situation is due to a variety of causes, but it is basically a direct heritage from the Renaissance and from the often bourgeois connections of Renaissance humanistic education. Unlike Continental Europe, where the humanist college (*collège, colegio*) grew up outside the university (more or less in opposition to the older institution, and rather soon finding itself an instrument of secondary education subordinated to the university), in the United States the college, an institution for secondary education of a more or less general sort, actually grew up into a university. The oldest university in the United States, Harvard, was originally Harvard College; despite its ideological and loose historical connection with the colleges forming part of Cambridge University, Harvard was from the beginning, by its independent existence and its affinities with other nonuniversity Dissenters' schools for training a literate ministry, quite close to the extra-university college.

Because of the pattern of growing up into a university established by Harvard and the other similar early American foundations, the

United States is also one of the very few places in the world where ecclesiastically directed, Catholic universities have ever existed, or indeed were ever thought of as a real possibility, and the only place where such universities exist in any number. For here, following the American pattern grown out of the Renaissance, the institutions known two generations ago as Catholic "colleges"—which meant at that time university preparatory schools—have themselves simply grown up into universities, or at least into colleges in the modern American sense of the word, institutions which offer a selection of courses at the university level.

This pattern of growth has involved a radical change in the status of humanistic studies which merits explicit attention, since its loose ideological and historical connection with Renaissance humanism invites the making of equations with Renaissance humanistic studies which are often false and misleading.

The general effect of the peculiar growth of American universities has been to spread the teaching of literature to higher age groups and to a wider audience than those found where the *collège* system has developed outside and under the university structure, and where formal contact with literature, history, and philosophy, except for those specializing at the university in one or another of these subjects—and consequently ordinarily studying nothing else—ends when one is about eighteen. If this means that we are called on to teach humanistic subjects at a level somewhat more mature than that which obtains in Europe—whether we actually do teach at such a mature level is another thing—it also means that our level of approach to the humanities must by far exceed that of the Renaissance educator. (I understand by this the teacher of literature and of philosophy in the Renaissance, not the Renaissance savant writing for his colleagues.) In the Renaissance for the most part, even after the age of Erasmus, literature as literature was seldom taught except to very small boys. With the end of the rhetoric course—or, as it came in part to be called, the humanities—at the age of fourteen or fifteen, the boy put aside literature, which had been all Latin with a sprinkling of Greek, for his scientific studies, starting with logic and natural philosophy, or, as we should say today, the physical sciences. Even these studies, which included philosophy, were finished commonly around the age of seventeen.[26]

The large-scale effort to teach literature to young men and young women in their late teens and early twenties is distinctive not of the Renaissance but of the twentieth century, and particularly of twentieth century America. If this fact runs contrary to what we think are the forces at work in American life, it would be well to revise our notion of these forces to conform to the facts. Erasmus ambitioned something like this (always excepting the young women, who were supposed generally not to be interested in literature at all, save the love literature in the vernacular); in this sense and with many reservations, the humanist ambitions of Erasmus are better fulfilled in the twentieth century American university than they were in his own day. The reservations to be made are, first, that Erasmus would have repudiated the whole present-day educational program because it is not concerned exclusively with the Latin, Greek, and Hebrew classics and because it is not taught, from the beginning of grade school on up, in Latin; and, second, that our elementary and secondary-school training in languages in America is regularly crude in the extreme, by any acceptable standards.

However, despite this handicap, the fact is that the context in which literature is approached within the educational system in the United States as compared to that within the Renaissance milieu is a context of relative maturity, at least with regard to the students' mere numerical age. Now, it is a fact that, while education necessarily involves both indoctrination and the development of a

[26] See George E. Ganss, S.J., *Saint Ignatius' Idea of a Jesuit University* (Milwaukee: Marquette University Press, 1954), pp. 44–80, especially p. 45. Peter Ramus brags that, instead of producing an M.A. at around the age of nineteen or twenty as the ordinary Paris course did, his own Collège de Presles was turning out M.A.'s, "not just in name but in reality and truth" (*non nomine sed revera ac veritate*), at the age of fifteen—Ramus, *Pro philosophica Parisiensis academiae disciplina oratio* (1551) in his *Scholae in liberales artes* (Basle, 1569), cols. 1019, 1044–47. The master of arts, of course, was supposed to have done all philosophy. Ramus' boys finished their rhetoric at about the age of twelve—which meant the end of their formal acquaintance with literature, although Ramus' practice of mingling "eloquence" with "philosophy" called nominally for literary skill in the "use," but not in the teaching, even of mathematics.

mature and open mind, younger students require proportionately more indoctrination and older students proportionately more encouragement not simply to acquire facts but to see large problems in all their fullness, even when the best answers devisable are incomplete. Maturity is not achieved until a person has the ability to face with some equanimity into the unknown. The approach to literature in the Renaissance curriculum was one largely accommodated to indoctrination. For the Renaissance humanist, literature was a *fait accompli,* a box in which the knowledge of the ancients was somehow stored.

There was, indeed, a sense of literature as purveying wisdom and as communicating enthusiasm. It was not forgotten that poetry came from ecstasy and inspiration, from a divine madness, and that the pursuit of literature was something best symbolized by the cult of those perennially fascinating and eternally evanescent figures, the Muses, whose invisible footprints on the sands of time M. Gilson has plotted in his recent brilliant volume. But what was lacking to the Renaissance, from the twentieth century point of view, was a sense of literature as exploratory, as facing into the unknown. A Gertrude Stein or a James Joyce, tinkering with the very structure of language to see what new and unexpected beauties it could be made to yield, would be rather unthinkable to the age of Colet and More, or even to that of Donne and Herbert. The notion that literature had before it indefinitely expanding horizons, and the related notion that the business of the writer was a kind of "sincerity," an objectivity in reporting which could lead to the discernment of issues previously unattended to or occluded, was hardly present.

It is, of course, true that the Renaissance developed a sense of history which the Middle Ages lacked. But this sense was largely a feeling for perspective regarding the past. There was little sense of the forward movement of history, of the present as a point on a trajectory traveling off into a future whose precise shape we do not know. What glimmerings there are of this kind of vision—as in Francis Bacon or perhaps Vico—are not felt as applying to literature. In short, there is no really widespread feeling for literary history. There is a feeling for what literature was or had been, not for what it might become or was becoming. The feeling for the future was defective, for the old pre-Christian cyclic view of history had never been effectively exorcized from men's minds. In this view, one thought of knowledge as recovery rather than as advance.

In a profound and mysterious sense, all knowledge is a kind of recovery, and it would be the height of folly to face into the future without knowing where one has come from out of the past. Still, too much adulation of the notion of a renaissance may lead us to forget that there is no way to avoid facing into the future, and that the more mature approach to literature which we today are called on to teach, at least in the upper reaches of the curriculum, demands precisely a facing into the unknown, of which the future is as good a symbol as any. We are called on to cultivate and to communicate to our more mature students an attitude which sees literature not as simply a refuge or solace but as a part of our unfinished world, where the unknown is faced and decisions made and the work of the Incarnation and Redemption thus carried on.

This point of view demands certain reservations in our attitudes toward Renaissance humanism, some of whose perspectives will have to be drastically reset if they are to be meaningful today. From the point of view of educators, if not of savants, one difficulty with the Renaissance classical heritage, of which F. R. Leavis has constantly and justifiably complained, was that its association of the study of literature almost exclusively with one's early teens has in the past made the cultivation of literature for many a means of refusing intellectual maturity and of confirming themselves in a state of perpetual, if uneasy, adolescence. To those influenced by this view, literature becomes a means of escape to the golden days of youth and intellectual irresponsibility. The horizons of literature if not defined by *The Owl and the Pussy-Cat,* at least do not extend beyond Dickens or perhaps Bret Harte. Even works which merit better treatment, such as the *Iliad* or Horace's *Satires,* are valued in this mood, by people capable of better things, not for what they really are, but for their association with one's school days and with perhaps one's private avatar of Mr. Chips which lurks in the memory. To this mind, literature is not of a piece with the equipment with which one faces actuality—indeed, one wonders whether this mind ever faces actuality anywhere at all. T. S. Eliot is read only when he has become accepted and his ideas old enough, some of them, to find their way into *Punch* and the *Saturday Evening Post*. For one has never been introduced to literature as an actuality unfolding itself constantly, as something living in history, but only as a source of indoctrination and of a few elemental emotional responses.

If there is to be a live humanism in letters today among Americans, Catholic or other, it must be approached somehow in a more mature framework than this. Literature must be viewed not as a means of indulging nostalgia for the past—either that of the human race or that of one's own youth—but as an initiation to the twentieth century and to the past as present here and as facing into the future. The Renaissance could, after all, taken in the large, deceive itself concerning its commitments to the present and future. It half believed in an earlier Golden Age of artistic achievement to which retreat might be advocated. This half-belief fed the approach which tended to think of literature principally as a source of indoctrination. But the human race itself, in some mysterious way, matures by living its way through time, and our sense of history—which is a sense of maturity—has advanced beyond what it was: we know that there never was such an age. The present cannot be left out of the accounting even in an approach to the past, for absolutes are not found simply by trekking back through the years. There can be no mature appreciation of any point in past artistic or literary achievement independent of an ability to identify and evaluate corresponding points in the present. The scholar who finds the twentieth century less comprehensible than the sixteenth certainly understands very little of the sixteenth. Of course, the converse is true: one's understanding of the present is proportionate to one's understanding of the past which is part of it. The double vision is essential: past and present, and the two faced into the future. In so far as they failed, the Renaissance humanists failed where they did not join these perspectives.

There is no doubt that in America and among Catholics a new humanism is needed, and one which has an entirely new orientation toward history from that of the Renaissance. There are huge issues to be faced, among the most notable that of communications in the mass society in which we are born and live, and that of the role of the machine and associated phenomena which must be integrated in our civilization into any humanism we propose to live. There is, of course, no neat and clear-cut set of answers available to us in handling these issues, because they are not clear, abstract problems which can be fitted with neat answers, but concrete issues which simply have to be lived with. In facing them, one thing is certain: although we can and must learn from the past, we cannot turn back, and we should not even dream of turning back. To this extent, Renaissance humanism is clearly passé. Christianity, a world view which, unlike other religions, bases its teachings on a real sacred *history*, has overcome the Renaissance and, by our day, imparted its outlook to the whole of mankind, so that now even non-Christian and anti-Christian cultures live in a linear rather than in a circular time, in an attitude of expectation, faced toward the future, when, as we know, Christ will come again.

If this is true of the world at large, it is doubly true of America. And if it is true of America, it should be doubly true of Catholics here. We are the people of the future in the land of the future. To be sure, our heritage stretches far back into the past. It is Renaissance and medieval and much more. But there is no solution for our dilemmas there. The dialectic of medieval and Renaissance only points up the dialectic of specialized, scientific training and of nonspecialized, liberal education which must be faced in every age, and more urgently than ever in our own. It would be a mistake if we failed to see these issues squarely. There is some danger, I believe, that Catholic intellectuals—or those who should be Catholic intellectuals—may be tempted to take refuge not in history but simply in the past. A true evaluation of the Renaissance may help us overcome this temptation.

5

TECHNOLOGY AND NEW HUMANIST FRONTIERS

In a common, popular view, the present age of technology is interpreted in terms of the "secularization" of society. This secularization is purported to have occurred first in Western society and to have spread or to be spreading thence into the other societies of the world. In this perspective the Middle Ages constituted the "age of Catholic faith," and the present age constitutes the "age of the machine," which obviously can have no faith, and which presumably infects its masters with its own soullessness.

So far as it goes, this interpretation of the age of technology is serviceable and in a sense true. But it is an extremely limited interpretation, made possible only by taking an exceedingly parochial view of the universe and of time and of history. For it is possible to see the Middle Ages as the great "age of Catholic faith" only if we are willing to write off the greater part of mankind, who were not and are not Europeans, and who had no available external contact with the Catholic faith at all. To think of a time when most of the human race had no contact whatsoever with the Church's teaching as a genuinely "Catholic" age is not only parochial but definitely scandalous. It suggests that Christ came to save not the human race but one's own family.

Evidence of such thinking can be discerned in such things as the presence of Gothic churches through the Orient, and some of its consequences in the tendency of various nativist movements, such as some in Central and South America, to become anti-Catholic in the process of being merely non-European. Such thinking is necessarily insidious, for it understands as an ideal type of Catholic existence an existence which was possible only because of its undesirable limitations. Yet it is certain that a great deal of contemporary Catholic thinking and activity is still dominated, most often subconsciously, and rendered ineffective by the notion that somehow conditions will necessarily be re-established through which nations will form solid blocs in which more or less everyone is nominally Catholic—a situation which obtained for only about three or four centuries over perhaps one-thirtieth of the earth's surface. To be sure, the medieval experience of Western Europe has had world-wide consequences so momentous that its importance as a historical reality can hardly be overestimated. But its relevance as a model for present-day Catholic activity and a framework for Catholic thought is, at best, highly suspect.

In a very real sense, the faith is more apparently and unmistakably Catholic today than it ever was in the "age of faith." Today there *are* Catholics in every country of the globe. They are scattered, but their lines of communication with one another and thus their awareness of one another are far more active and, in this sense, their cohesion is more real than that of earlier Catholics living in much greater geographical proximity. The unique position of the Holy Father as head of the Church is much more obvious than ever before. The faith has become more explicit on innumerable important points—many medieval Catholics, for example, felt quite convinced that Our Lady was conceived in original sin—and the faith has been disengaged from entanglements with errors of early physical science. Doubtless in our minds it is entangled with certain scientific errors of our own age, but at least some of the old ones have been eliminated: we are not inclined to believe, as many earlier Catholics were, that we cannot accept divine Revelation without believing that the sun goes around the earth!

This kind of progress—for it is progress—going on within the interior of the Church herself suggests the impoverishment of the view which would interpret postmedieval history chiefly in terms of progressive "secularization" of everything and would see the development of modern science which began in the sixteenth and seventeenth centuries and leads into our present age of technology as, at best, one of the less deplorable incidents in this secularization.

To make the modern world and world view, much more than "secularization" has, quite obviously, been going on. Seen in larger historical, and prehistorical, perspectives, the age of technology is part of the great and mysterious evolution of the universe devised by God. It can be considered as an epoch in what we may call the "hominization" of the world, that is, the taking over of our planet by mankind.

II

Until a few generations ago, men commonly regarded the world as embodying relationships which were basically static. Mankind was thought of as settled in a pattern of existence where the relationships between himself and the cosmic forces around him remained quite invariable. The universe itself was thought of as extraordinarily constant. In the Aristotelian cosmology, nothing above the lunar sphere was subject to any real alteration at all. The hollow spheres in which were set the planets and finally the stars moved with a perfect circular motion without the possibility of other change. The earth and everything on it was compounded of the four elements: earth, water, air, and fire. It was commonly thought that men tilled it and worked on it as they had always tilled it and worked on it, until they were replaced by a new generation, which found its relationships with nature quite the same as those of its forebears.

Now we know that the relationships between man and the universe are by no means entirely static. We live in an evolving and expanding universe, and man's relationships with it are in many ways radically different today from what they were a hundred thousand years ago, or even ten thousand years ago, or even a hundred years ago. Much of the story of the universe is written in the rocks beneath our feet, and still more in the readings which we can take from the stars. In both these records, we discern a forward movement, a development, an evolution which is apparently irreversible and which in geology is charted in terms of the various geological ages, following one after the other in a mysterious, but unmistakably patterned, sequence. Taking as a frame of reference the vast expanses of time and of space which modern study of the cosmos and of our globe has revealed, I should like here to consider our technological age, in only a very few of its most generalized aspects, as one of the geological epochs, that is, as something belonging to this particular time in the pattern of events which constitutes the development of the natural world. All this will be not without theological implications, for it is in this natural world, again at a certain epoch and at no other, that the Second Person of the Blessed Trinity, who like His Father and the Holy Spirit is the One God, entered into the evolutionary pattern by becoming one of us, a true Man.

According to several convergent methods of computation, the age of the universe appears to be perhaps some 5,000,000,000 years. The blob of matter which in this universe makes up our own earth was in its early ages quite uninhabitable for any form of life. But by what is known as the Archeozoic Pre-Cambrian era, something like 2,000,000,000 years ago and some 3,000,000,000 years from the calculated beginning of our universe, despite the great volcanic activity which persisted, probably certain microscopic algae and some protozoa had appeared and life on earth had begun. Some 1,000,000,000 years later, in the Proterozoic Pre-Cambrian era, the first sponges had appeared, and animal life was well on its way, but it was not until roughly another 500,000,000 years in the Ordovician period, which is thus a little less than 500,000,000 years ago, that the first vertebrates seem to have developed. In the Silurian and Devonian periods, the great age of the fishes, between 300,000,000 and 390,000,000 years ago, the first dry-land plants and animals evolved from their pelagic ancestors and the land masses of the world began to be populated with living things.

These periods are followed by others remarkable for their characteristic life forms: the Carboniferous period, characterized by the development of the huge, luxuriant plant life which is now transformed into what we call coal; the Permian, Triassic, and Jurassic periods, in which reptiles dominate the scene, developing eventually into the incredibly massive dinosaurs, which after some 50,000,000 more years become extinct, as the huge carboniferous plants had become extinct; the Cretaceous period, in which about 100,000,000 years ago the first mammals, relatively tiny things, appear, followed immediately by the Tertiary period, in which the mammals quickly rise to dominance—quickly, because our denominators of change have now shrunk from the billions to the tens of millions of years, that is, to one one-hundredth of their earlier size. Finally, somewhere in the Pleistocene epoch, which began some 1,000,000 years ago (whether in the very early or the later Pleistocene is not indisputably clear at present) the paleontological record reveals the presence of the first men.

In this development, we can discern a certain unmistakable pattern, a forward movement or "evolution" whereby a world with at first nothing more than brute matter held together by the forces of gravity and inertia becomes subject more and more to the claims of life, and in such a way that, despite incidental retrogressions, the kind of life becomes successively higher and higher—taking man always as our standard of comparison—more and more, that is to say, like that of the human body which crowns this development as the physical organism finally adapted to substantial union with the individually created, immortal human soul. There is, in this sense, in the pattern which created material existence describes through time, a gradual spiritualizing momentum.

III

But there is something more to note in this pattern. It exhibits a kind of greater and greater acceleration. The crucial developments —or at least those which look crucial to us, for we are, after all, human beings, and our perspective is *the* perspective for the material world below us—appear at first scaled by the billions, next by the millions, and finally by mere hundreds of thousands of years.

Of course, we may suspect that this scaling is arbitrary, for is it not inevitable that we should know more about the ages which are closer to ourselves and thus have a greater number of meaningful divisions into which we can break them down? If we knew as much detail about the Archeozoic Pre-Cambrian era as we do about the Cenozoic era, and about the physiology and ecology of the Archeozoic protozoa as we do about the physiology and ecology of the modern mammals, would we not be able to divide the Archeozoic into significant 100,000-year units? The argument is that the earlier eras and periods and epochs could be more broken down or differentiated if we only knew more about them, so that they, too, would exhibit truly crucial events every few hundred thousand years.

But this argument for differentiation in the earlier eras loses its force when we remember that it is precisely *differentiation itself* which is originating in the development we are charting. In the primitive life forms there are no differences quite comparable to those between the horse and the amoeba—only perhaps the foundation for such differences in some obscure physiological or even chemical change which is important, to be sure, but which manifests its importance only *in much later eras* when *life is sufficiently differentiated* to give a finely calibrated scale against which to measure such differences. In other words, the hypothetical minuscule physiological change which took place in a certain strain of Archeozoic protozoan and thereby made possible the evolution of the modern horse was important not to the Archeozoic protozoan, which, *for the moment, went on living much as before*, but *to the horse.*

That is to say, if any fine scaling is introduced into earlier eras, it is projected back into them out of the actually finely scaled recent world. Fine scaling does not belong to the early days of creation and of evolution. It is in the nature of things that if we use hundreds of thousands of years for more recent events, we should use for the earlier events billions of years. For if the position of the observer must be taken into account, nevertheless there is no other position to take the observations from than that of the observer. The earlier, less differentiated periods have their meaning in terms of those sufficiently differentiated for man to exist in them.

The situation is something like that in Einstein's calculations regarding the motion of stellar systems. If star B and star C are receding from star A in exactly opposite directions each at two-thirds the speed of light, an observer on star B will not see star C as receding from him at twice two-thirds or four-thirds the speed of light, but would compute this velocity as rather less than the speed of light. Similarly, our paleontological measurements cannot be calculated nor accurately imagined independent of a specific observer, for what you are measuring is a series of changes calculated to prepare for the observer, that is, for man.

IV

What we have been describing provisionally as a temporal speedup is in fuller perspective a kind of cumulative intensification of the movement whereby life has been "taking over" our globe. It is cumulative because each stage inherits the acquisitions of the preceding stage and has proportionately more reserves for activity. The late Father Pierre Teilhard de Chardin liked to style the three great epochs of our earth's existence those respectively of the "geosphere," when the globe was held together only by mechanical forces; the "biosphere," when it achieved a new unity in the envelope of organic life which it threw around itself; and the "noosphere," when it achieved a new unity, which while transcendent was nevertheless natural to it, that which it knows within the *nous* or mind of man. Each of these stages not only builds on and transcends the other, but because of this very fact has a greater store of energy to draw on to perfect itself. Thus, if it took some three billion years before the earliest plant and animal life formed on the geosphere and thereby transmuted this geosphere into a biosphere, it took the biosphere rather less time to prepare itself for the advent of man, when it was transmuted into the noosphere. The advent of man was proportionately an even greater event than the advent of life. And yet it was accomplished in less time, being worked out against a far richer and more complex reserve of activity; namely, that of the biosphere.

The noosphere is richer and more subtle and more complex than what has gone before it. It is far from static. For within it, too, patterns of intensification can be observed, more rapid, more venturesome because at the same time more conservative, and more momentous in the long run, because these patterns are developed through the actions of free spiritual beings.

Man's efforts to take possession of the earth are at first desperately slow. Scattered eolithic hunters spread over a few areas of the earth apparently for tens or hundreds of thousands of years, knowing little beyond their own horizon, although knowing that, to be sure, in a way entirely transcending that of the beasts. Then the more advanced paleolithic and neolithic ages come, terminating in the great civilizations of Egypt around the year 4000 B.C. From this point on, the intensification is tremendous. The changes between the First Dynasty and Julius Caesar took less than 4,000 years, and the vast changes between Caesar's world and our own have come about in only 2,000.

In a sense, it is true, once an intelligent, spiritual being appears on earth, there is no change at all. For each spiritual being is a universe in himself, a microcosm, and an absolute, with an interior of consciousness impenetrable to others in which upon his death he will have to meet alone with God. But in terms of the globe, and in terms of man's own place in it—for, after all, he has a place in it, and this place is important for the globe and for other men—the change is momentous.

We are speaking here not merely of changes in material culture, but of these changes as they affect men's spiritual, intellectual, and moral relation to the universe, to his past and future, and to other men. It is our persuasion that changes in material culture cannot but affect the spiritual world, for actually they are initiated there. They are not merely material and cannot be. Effected by man in a definite pattern of development which knows no real reversal, they are changes within the "noosphere" itself—the globe as unified by means of the presence in it of rational animals, the globe as possessed by the mind of man.

The situation here can be seen in sharp focus in those developments which center around communication. Thousands upon thousands of years after man's appearance on earth, at a time somewhat less than 4,000 years ago, various forms of picture writing or of other recorded expression were finally supplemented by the alphabet. Invented only once in the entire global history of mankind—for all alphabets from the Hebrew and Roman to the Sanskrit and Korean are descended from the original Semitic—this alphabet spread to the four corners of the world, dramatizing in its own case history the function of the arts of communication in uniting man, and through him the world, in a growing self-consciousness. Man had prepared himself for perhaps as long as 1,000,000 years for this invention. Yet it took only some three millennia more for the invention of printing with letters of the alphabet made in movable type cast from matrices struck from a punch. It took only a few hundred more years for the invention of the telegraph, then less than half a century for the wireless. A few decades more were required for television. The rapidity of development, or, better, the growing intensity of development in means of communication here makes us think that the present age is unique. Actually, it is in a profound sense not unique at all, for it is continuing the pattern of increased acceleration and intensity in development set by preceding eras.

From the beginning in pictographs and the alphabet itself, and most particularly in the case of printing, the development of means of communication has been largely a matter of mechanics. Yet the term of these mechanical developments has not been "material" in its most significant sense at all. It has been spiritual and it has been humanistic, if we mean by humanistic centered upon distinctively human interests or ideals, having to do with man's interests as a man. At the term of these developments in communication, men are more in touch with one another and life has more fully taken possession of the entire globe than ever before. The process which was initiated when the first men began to spread out over the earth by dint of locomotion and, consequently by learning of the earth to possess it through their intelligence, to give it a wholeness and unity which it cannot have outside the "noosphere," outside the consciousness of a spiritual being, has come to a relatively advanced stage. Within the past few generations, through the newspaper and the radio and now through television, thinking men the world over have at least some of the vital happenings from all over the surface of the globe presented to them as readily and as promptly as if they had happened a mile or so away.

This is not purely spiritual achievement, but its spiritual aspects, and still more its spiritual potentialities, are tremendous. If it induces a certain exteriorism by leading us to think of life in terms of reportable exterior events, it also means in unmistakable, if limited, ways a gain in self-consciousness and self-possession on the part of the human race as a whole, and hence a gain in interiority.

At the same time, this development in means of communication has been a matter of technology. Indeed, it focuses the relationship of technology and culture in its most humanistic aspects. The great humanists of the Renaissance—the Manutii, Sturm, the Amerbachs, Froben, Oronce Fine, members of St. Thomas More's circle—were often enough printers. This fact is more relevant to the modern world of technology than it is often taken to be, for the printing press marked the beginning of the age of technology not only because it made possible the rapid diffusion of information which such an age demanded but even more because it was itself the first effective assembly line. For the first really mass-produced object was not a machine or a gadget, but a book. It is one of the surprises of real history that, when men took to stamping out carefully wrought objects which were exact copies of one another, the first things they taught themselves to stamp out on a large scale were not tools or gadgets but representations in space of their thoughts. Whatever its difficulties, mass production was invented to serve spiritual needs.

This is an astonishing and revealing fact regarding the relationship of technology to human life and development. It does away, or should do away, for all time with unreal oppositions between "technology" on the one side and "humanistic views" on the other. There is, of course, some kind of opposition between technology and humanism—there is opposition between any two things which are not the same—but the opposition is not the kind of horrible thing which is often implied. The very term "technology" is a product of the nontechnological world and advertises the connection between this world and technology itself. In philosophers of the sixteenth and seventeenth centuries, particularly those who, like William Ames, were followers of Peter Ramus, "technology" or *technologia* is at first a treatise on any one of the liberal arts organized "logically" or according to the rules of that particular liberal art called logic. From this semantic area, technology migrates to cover similar treatises on the mechanical arts, and then further to cover the application of scientific knowledge to industrial or other practical uses. But etymologically and historically, and hence really, to conceive of the modern world as dominated by "technology" is to conceive of it as organized by analogy with the *liberal* arts!

The picture of the universe which we have so inadequately and amateurishly attempted to sketch here is far from being fully assimilated by the human sensibility, American, European, or other. It is too new in our consciousness. Primitive man lived for myriads of years apparently with no more knowledge of his own history than that enshrined in legends and myths. His knowledge of "real" history of man or of the universe in any twentieth century sense could hardly have extended beyond one or two or three generations. By the time of the Egyptians and the Mayas historical penetration of the past had improved, and by the time of the Hebrews and of the Greeks Thucydides and Herodotus or the Roman historians, history in something like our modern sense was known, if for a very limited span of time. The Renaissance knew an accurate history reaching back more than two thousand years before the age of the Renaissance itself. By the nineteenth century, with Lyell and Darwin and others, the frontiers of the past were being pushed indefinitely further. Only within the past twenty-five years have we been able to gain our present insights into the lives of the stars and the vaster reaches of space, and to understand that in looking at the stars we are literally seeing the occurrence of events which took place many millions and even billions of years ago and which have taken all this time to send their light to us.

Man's penetration of the past here is another instance of the intensification of his activity in taking possession of the world about which we have already spoken. In this case the intensification of his study of the past which has grown with the millennia has increased his recuperative powers so that the twentieth century, which is the time at present most removed from the creation of the world, has the greatest fund of naturally acquired knowledge bearing on the creation that man has ever known.

V

However, if the age of technology is part of a long sequence of cosmic development, and if technology itself has discernible connections with the liberal arts, the coexistence of modern technology and a view of life which is militantly humanistic—dedicated to distinctively human interests and ideals—does pose problems. These problems are by no means entirely new. They are remarkably like those posed when Renaissance humanism arose to confront the scholastic tradition, for, compared with Renaissance humanism in its literary and artistic focus, scholasticism represents the scientific and even technological approach to reality and to life.

In the set-to between this humanism and scholasticism, it was impossible for humanism to win a clear-cut victory. For the Renaissance man had a scholastic past, even when he rebelled against it, and it was not too long until his stress on language study became a stress on scientific and even technological language study. Indeed, it was man as trained by the Renaissance who finally produced the modern technological world, so that to this extent the Renaissance not only succumbed to, but actually ended by propagating, the scientism against which it had rebelled. On the other hand, because the Renaissance had attacked a too abstract, formalistic, scientific approach to life, when such an approach was re-formed after the Renaissance, it could no longer be so sure of itself as, in some of its aspects, pre-Renaissance scholasticism was. Technology ever after would tend to be on the defensive, suspicious of its own achievements. This seems to be where we are today.

But if our present conditions are related to and comparable to those of the Renaissance, they are also infinitely more complicated. For in revising our knowledge of the universe and in situating man in it, technology has entered more intimately into our most interior perspectives. For our present knowledge of the universe—and I take it that knowledge of the universe is now, as it was in ancient times, intellectually liberating—we are most intimately dependent on technology. It is technology which has made possible the telescopes of Mount Wilson and Palomar and the entirely new radio telescopes, with the vast accumulation of liberal and intellectually liberating knowledge which they have made available concerning the cosmos we live in. In the study of the origins of life and of early human life, technology and Geiger counters help to date our fossils and to detect occasional frauds such as that of the "Piltdown Man." More and more, technology is proving invaluable in the study of that most human and most elusive of all phenomena, language itself. In these cases, and in the myriads of others where it comes into play, technology is not everything. It provides tools—but let us own frankly that they are essential tools, without which some critically illuminating insights would be utterly impossible.

Far from being "opposed" in any *simpliste* manner to a view of the universe centered on man, technology has been necessary in order for us to have learned what little we know about tremendously important details of man's place in the universe. Moreover, as we have seen, it has made possible advances in communication which are essential to man's "occupation" of this planet, to man's taking over the planet from the forces of brute, nonintellectual nature. Technology is an incident in the history of mankind. It is something interior to this history, not exterior. Any cultural view which pretends to be humanistically centered thus has no choice at all about dealing with technology. It has to deal with technology, for technology is a great and inspiring human creation.

The failure of humanistic culture in the face of technology, in so far as there has been a failure—for I am not at all convinced that there is any extraordinary failure so far—has been a failure of humanistic culture to enlarge itself enough to include the technological age in its view. Too often there has been a battle against technology rather than an effort to view technology humanistically. Technology cannot be "conquered" and eliminated. History never reverses itself. Let us remember the Renaissance humanists' mistake. The prescholastic age of which they dreamed never returned. Their very attacks on scholasticism, argumentative and sparked by the notion that language must be subject to external, static control, reveal them as postscholastic men. Similarly, the modern polemicists who take up arms against the sea of technology reveal themselves as technologists of history, viewing history as a machine which can be thrown into reverse. The cause of humanism is served by dealing with reality, not by denouncing it. Only if technology can be interpreted in terms of man and man's career in the universe, past, present, and future, can the age of technology be dealt with humanistically at all.

It is of course not easy to effect this interpretation, and the failure to do so has so far been both historical and theological—perhaps one in being the other. The historical *significance* of this technological era in terms of what we have called the "hominization" of the planet has not been sufficiently explored, and the meaning of this "hominization" in terms of Catholic theology, which is the only theology that includes history and is not included by it, has been distressingly neglected.

The task of interpretation here is a tremendous one for the Catholic mind. For if the technological age is of major importance in the "hominization" of the universe, this "hominization" itself reaches its apogee by being at once realized and transcended in the Person of Christ, the God-Man, Who is at once the most perfect man, and more than man, God Himself. The "hominization" of the universe partially accomplished before Christ's coming was a preparation for Him. This "hominization" was a condition of the Incarnation, which had to be an event of the "noosphere" rather than of the "geosphere" or of the "biosphere." For the Incarnation would be meaningless without reference to the universe as understood by man. Following His coming and His work of redemption, the increasingly intensified "hominization" of the globe is in a very real way His own work, for only as this "hominization" progresses can the world as a whole more and more return to Him in that "restoration" of all things through and in Christ which is not a return to any real condition of a previous era but which will be accomplished for the first and the last time at the end of time.

That, even after Christ, this "hominization" of our globe is not necessarily its Christianization goes without saying, for incorporation into Christ or perseverance in this incorporation is a matter of grace freely offered by God. To be sure, grace operates in the world only in so far as man is present. It touches the universe through the "noosphere," which is to say through men's minds and souls. In this sense, the evolution of the cosmos prepares the ground for revelation. Still, cosmic evolution is not in a direct line leading to supernatural salvation. The processes involved in it not only may be put to evil uses, but actually, through man, bear the mark of original sin. It is significant that, just as man's original use of his gift of freedom was for ends which were not intended by God and which involved the race in catastrophe, so the original use of our most spectacularly great recent discovery, atomic energy, was to kill and maim. The mark of sin is upon man, and upon the universe through him. Still, the "hominization" of the globe, its being taken over by men, is a good, in the way in which the "nature" with which the supernatural works is good. The better and the more advanced nature is, the more there is for the supernatural to affect.

VI

If cosmic evolution as it shows itself on our planet is thus not inevitably "progress" in the sense that it does not better human nature, still it is progress in so far as it comes to term in the greater and greater "hominization" of the globe, in so far as it focuses all activity on this planet more and more in man, where the greatest possibilities for perfectibility—as well as for evil—lie. Insight into the significance of this "hominization" of the cosmos, now that we are aware that it is taking place, must be among the objectives of any realistic humanism, for it indicates the outlines of a large-scale natural activity in which human life is involved. Only within the framework of this "hominization" process can the technological age be understood.

This understanding requires at least two things: First, there must be a general awareness, varying with each one's own cultural position and achievements, of technology as fitting in the time-pattern of human development and as growing out of earlier human achievements, poetic, artistic, literary, philosophical, and religious. The way to this is being prepared by the studies, under way for some two generations now and gradually penetrating the collective consciousness, on the origins of our modern scientific mind, for these studies show more and more the connection of scientific thinking with a whole constellation of attitudes registered in the other non-scientific achievements of the human spirit. Secondly, there must be an awareness, related to and almost presupposed by the first, of what the larger pattern of "hominization" in the universe has been and signifies. For the Catholic, this must include a realization of the meaning of the Incarnation and Redemption in cosmic history. For the Catholic theologian particularly, the knowledge of an evolving universe gained in the nineteenth century thus poses a formidable task which must begin with a humble attempt to learn what cosmic history has really been, and must proceed—for it will never properly end—to the integration of this understanding, with all the fresh and totally unexpected insights and problems which it has to offer, into revelation, and to the tremendous enriching of Christology which such integration promises.

One might add that for the American consciousness, a peculiar urgency here obtains. For while it is only boorish even to suggest that the United States is more civilized than other countries, American or European or Asiatic, for she is not, the fact remains that her relationship to technology is a special one. In the United States the technological developments of all the nations are in a way focused and intensified. To this extent, America is a special avant-garde point in the "hominization" of our planet, and her problems are those of the whole human race, only in concentrated form.

For a real humanism of the technological age, no one can offer an easy, ready-made plan. Any such humanism depends on our growing into a profound knowledge of the roots which connect technology with man. This means living with a sense of our own history and of that of the universe.

Our purpose has been here to suggest that technology, like anything else new, must be faced not in the spirit of nostalgia but in the historical spirit. A kind of cosmic nostalgia, the desire somehow to escape from history, is an old pagan disease. There is nothing Christian in it. The Church in her teaching and in her liturgy shows no signs of nostalgia. She does not dream of a Golden Age to which she longs to return. For her, the Second Adam is infinitely better than the first. Man after the Fall, sinful but redeemed by Christ, is better off than before the Fall. *O felix culpa,* the Church sings in her solemn liturgy on Holy Saturday. The fact that so often her members show signs of a cosmic nostalgia, reluctance to face what history brings and to welcome it, shows that they, to that extent, have failed to free themselves from their pagan past which dogs us all and undoubtedly will dog all Christians—perhaps to an ever diminishing extent—to the end of time.

The same discoveries which have brought us the perspectives suggested by this treatment have also brought to Christians the explicit awareness of a fact which has long been with them: the fact that the Christian is at home in history and in a forward-moving, developing universe, whereas the pagan, radically, is not. The full implications of this fact remain to be elaborated by Catholic theology. Indeed, this elaboration of a Christology of an evolving universe seems to be the great task before modern and in a particular way before American theologians. It is a task which, unfortunately, they have hardly begun. But only in their setting themselves to it will the pattern of a technological humanism emerge. For the problem of technology is, at root, a religious and a theological one.

6

THE FAITH, THE INTELLECTUAL, AND THE PERIMETERS

THE EFFECTIVE CATHOLIC intellectual has commonly been situated on the Church's perimeter, between the Faith and its surroundings. This is noteworthy even in the case of St. Paul and St. John the Evangelist, the most intellectual or speculative of the New Testament writers. Paul in great part deals with the frontier between New Testament teaching and the pre-New-Testament mind, John with the frontier between New Testament teaching and Hellenized Judaism—the latter itself a phenomenon of the frontier between reason and revelation.

The special intermediary role of the intellectual in the economy of Revelation is even more evident when one turns to the major noninspired figures. St. Augustine's importance to Christian culture, like that of the Greek Fathers and thinkers on whom he draws, exists in terms of his success in fecundating with the truths of Christianity the rhetorical tradition which had summed up the pagan achievement. Similarly, the significance of St. Albert the Great and St. Thomas Aquinas centers upon their assimilating to the Christian tradition the Aristotle who even in Albert's and Thomas' own day was forbidden in the University of Paris curriculum and some of whose most basic doctrines—no creation, no Providence, and perhaps no immortality for the human soul—will always remain radically and unalterably opposed to Catholic teaching.

Without quite sharing our present-day perspectives, St. Thomas Aquinas nevertheless hints at the special role of the intellectual in the Church when he suggests that the maximum achievement of the theologian can be only negative: theology exists to defend the faith from its enemies. That is to say, in the last analysis the intellect can never finally and positively explicate the mysteries of the Faith, but only deal with the potentially infinite objections *against* them. In a very real sense, at the center of Catholic life, there is nothing for the soul to do but, through Jesus Christ, to contemplate and love God, who needs no explanation but is Himself Explanation of all. All the explicatory work, the travail of the intellect which we ordinarily understand by the intellectual life, is peripheral to the central concern here. In this sense, the faith is speculatively neuter, and that possessed by the uneducated illiterate quite as acceptable as that of any bishop or theologian.

Nevertheless, peripheral activity around this quiet but not passive center of faith is necessary and obligatory. For, so long as the world endures in its present state, the mission which is the Incarnation and the Church is never concluded. Christ is continually in the state of being sent to the world, because the world is continuously becoming —which means that He is continually taking possession of what has heretofore not encountered His redemptive action. This taking possession must occur in the intellectual dimension as well as in the social or economic or any other dimension. Indeed, the intellect (with the will, which depends on it) being what it is, the crown of man's powers, Christ's taking possession of the realm of the intellect is in a way the most important and glorious of the works of the redemption. The taking possession cannot possibly be something realizable once for all. Rather, it is the matter of endless adjustment, accomplished within the dialectical movement—something best likened to a conversation between two persons—which governs the relation of the natural and the supernatural and manifests its living tensions in the kaleidoscope of uneasily paired terms which strew the path of Catholic intellectual history: St. Paul's freeman and slave, Jew and pagan, Christian and unconverted Jew, St.

Augustine's City of God and City of the World, the two swords of ecclesiastical and of civil authority.

In terms of the dialectic or dialogue between the City of God and the City of Man, the situation of the Catholic intellectual in the United States would seem particularly happy. The United States is a country of dialogue, or dialogues, a land of cultural pluralism, where Catholics are constantly rubbing elbows with those not of the Faith. One would expect that Catholic thought in the United States would have made great speculative advances and would have developed a certain intellectual suppleness and resilience. The fact that up to the present this has so little been the case, the fact that Catholic thought in America has commonly lagged behind that of European countries and has fought shy of contact with American intellectual movements, is a fact which needs some explanation, or at least comment.

II

It is commonly believed that there is something in the American temper or heritage, non-Catholic or Catholic, which is unfavorable to speculation. Nevertheless, there has been a great deal of intellectual activity in the United States within the past hundred years. The work of Josiah Royce, William James, Charles Sanders Peirce, Justice Holmes, John Dewey, Louis D. Brandeis, and many others cannot be brushed aside as insignificant. Moreover, the intellectual work of such men has been relevant not merely to the surroundings of the Church in America, to the milieu in which the Church in America is situated, but to the internal economy of the Church in America and to the real and tremendous achievement realized by American Catholics. In their educational procedures and aims, more practical and in many ways more successful socially than anything that Catholic or non-Catholic Continental Europe has ever been able to manage, American Catholics exhibit many of the very traits which a mind such as Dewey's set out to deal with and channel. It is of course evident that Catholics could not string along with Dewey's kind of naturalism, which has much in it diametrically opposed to the faith. Still, it is worthy of observation that, faced with their own behavior and the doctrines of Dewey which do something both to explain and to foster this behavior, they have felt called on to focus their attention on what was *wrong* in Dewey rather than to try to assess and assimilate his real contribution to America's understanding of herself.

This dominantly negative approach to Dewey has been only a part of the larger pattern of rejection which has commonly characterized Catholic theorists' reaction to the American environment, particularly in educational matters—a pattern of rejection which operates on the conscious theoretical level at the very time an opposed pattern of acceptance is operating, to good purpose and with wonderful effect, on the subconscious level. It is almost as though American Catholics had made up their minds to theorize not about their real modes of action but only about what they do not do or what they do under protest.

The results of the negative attitude in evidence here are, some of them, well known. Many American Catholics take evident pleasure in hearing themselves told by persons such as Robert Maynard Hutchins that they have capitulated too far to American educational objectives and procedures. But they often blink the fact that some of their finest achievements have resulted from their capitulations. American Catholic tourists roam the world looking, generally in vain, for fine parish schools like their own, unaware that it is the scorned leveling process in American education as well as the peculiarly American institution of coeducation which has made such schools possible for the first time in Catholic history. Among other things which it has done, coeducation has opened vast reserves of woman power for the teaching of boys in a maneuver unknown to more "traditional" and more illiterate Catholic cultures.

The unnecessary mystification of issues in evidence here has not been the only result of the tendency of Catholic theorists to approach America negatively. A more lamentable result has been that there is nowhere any comprehensive theory of Catholic education as realized or realizable on the American scene written by a Catholic out of any deep understanding of the significance of the United States and her own peculiar institutions—which Catholics have assimilated so well, and for which they actually have such positive and even chauvinist enthusiasm. While our practical energy has gone into the Church's tremendous contribution toward making America significant, our more specifically intellectual energy seems to have been regularly channeled into prescribing what was wrong with things, into "viewing with alarm."

Much of this situation has in truth, been inevitable, being due to the antagonism generated by reaction among Catholics as a minority group in a culture which has been in great part Protestant in orientation. The hostility of this culture, although usually more genteel than savage, and often paradoxically benevolent, has given a squint to Catholic thought in America which could lead Catholics to complacent intellectual suicide. "Students of philosophy," writes an American priest reviewing with typical approval a study of Stalin by another American priest, "should examine Stalin's ideas to discover their theoretical fallacies." That those who think merely of innoculating a popular culture against the evils of Communism should take this blindly negative approach is perhaps understandable. But that a student of philosophy, presumably a humble searcher for wisdom, should be so high-handed is, at the least, astonishing. One wonders where we would have been had St. Thomas set out to "examine Aristotle's ideas" simply "to discover their theoretical fallacies." St. Thomas, being not a philosopher but a theologian, would seem to have the maximum warrant for such procedure, in view of his defense-of-the-Faith outlook mentioned above, but his actual technique is far more humble and rewarding: he goes to Aristotle, at the time often popularly supposed to be the enemy of all that was Christian, to see if, even with all his major errors, Aristotle may perhaps know some things which Thomas does not.

III

Pride often attacks persons in terms of assets or riches which they actually possess. One way in which it can attack Catholics is by leading them to believe that they are dispensed from cultivating a humble curiosity about God's creation because by reason of their faith they have surety regarding their own relationship to God through Christ in His Church. This kind of attitude constitutes a permanent threat to the intellectual apostolate of the Church in all ages, but it is a particularly ominous threat in the United States today. For in the United States, intellectual isolationism is practicable for Catholics in ways in which it is not in many other countries, and, at the same time, the permanent problems of Catholic intellectual life, generated by the interaction of the Church with her environment, are in a way posed in the United States with an urgency greater at the present time than perhaps anywhere else in the world.

The reason for the practicability of isolationism in the United States is the freedom of the academic tradition from state domination. Catholic universities, as well as secondary schools, are in complete control of their own programs, setting their own examinations—unlike France, where all examinations, beginning with those for the *bachot* or high-school diploma, are set and administered on a nation-wide basis. Not only Catholic high schools and universities, but all high schools and universities in the United States, state-supported universities included, are scholastically autonomous, coming to an understanding with one another not through a common examining board, but rather by membership in voluntary, nongovernmental standardizing agencies, such as the North Central Association, which the universities and secondary schools, state-supported as well as privately supported, have set up themselves and which are so respected that very few first-rate institutions feel that they can exempt themselves from membership. The standardization enjoined by these agencies is less dictatorial and more flexible than most state-imposed standardization. Practically the only examinations encountered by any student not set up by the institution which he is attending are the examinations set by the individual state boards which one must pass to practice medicine or law in the state in question. Even these examinations, passed in one state, are not necessarily honored in another—for the United States remains radically a union of forty-eight sovereign republics.

The freedom from crushing centralization in evidence here is one of the most real and refreshing—and, to Europeans, one of the least known—aspects of American culture. Catholic educators are among the firmest believers in the many obvious advantages of this decentralized—and to a Frenchman chaotic—freedom, particularly in a country the size of the United States, where all centralization is commonly looked on as something to be avoided as much as is humanly possible. But if the autonomy of each educational unit has given the Church a freedom which she has enjoyed in few countries—notable exceptions being the British Empire and the Low Countries—it has also created the danger that the Catholic intellectual may find himself unable to carry on a dialogue with others because of unfamiliarity with their state of mind owing to lack of real intellectual contact.

Intellectual isolationism is all the more a threat for the Catholic in America because his business and social contacts with non-Catholics are so manifold. Precisely because there are so many contacts of this sort with Protestants and other non-Catholics to be exploited, the zealous Catholic is, more often than not, invited to minimize real intellectual developments and to think of intellectual issues largely at second hand in terms of carefully worked-out explanations with which "informed" Catholics are familiar.

This is all right except when one wants to develop a real intellectual life, which must, of necessity, have some sort of avant-garde formation—that is, a curiosity about questions which have as yet no answers worked out, or which have not even been formulated fruitfully as questions. It is a commonplace that the avant-garde of thought has an importance today greater than ever before. This is due not so much to the fact that the contemporary mind is revolutionary as to the fact that it is also highly conservative. With historical knowledge more accessible than ever before, at its best the contemporary mind, more than any earlier mind, feels its activity as taking place at a kind of wave front, for it feels the present as growing out of the past. This is why, as Père Jean Daniélou has so well put it, all thinking which does not have historical dimension, however true it may be, is simply ineffective today. Mathematics and mathematical physics itself are not exempt from the pressure of historical thinking. Einstein felt compelled to produce a book detailing the actual development of his theory of relativity in his own mind and that of his associates. For physical and mathematical discovery, too, takes place in time. There is a "front" even of the most abstract kind of thought. The human mind has, in our day, achieved an awareness of this age-old fact more explicit and acute than ever before.

IV

Because of America's special symbolic value in an economy of "fronts," the problem of the Church's interactions with her environment can be said to be posed in a way more urgently in the United States than it is anywhere else today. For the American Catholic intellectual, this awareness of thought as a front between the past and the future, sharpened by his general love for all frontiers which is part of his pioneer American heritage, reinforces, and is itself reinforced by, the position of Catholic intellectual activity on the front between Revelation and the natural world. His very religious commitments make him more than ever what every American secretly wishes to be or to have been (at least by proxy in his ancestors, real or fictitious): a frontiersman, a man situated where an active culture is thrusting forward at its periphery and effecting a transmutation of the areas with which it is surrounded.

To a certain extent, it is true, the sense of history is less explicit in the United States than in Continental Europe. The United States has preserved the more static, abstract, so-called "objective" interest in reality which the Anglo-Saxon world had already acquired in the Middle Ages, when it was producing so many more than its share of logicians. This interest contrasts with intellectual interests in Continental Europe, which has always remained rather closer to the tradition of a real dialectic or dialogue, or even rhetoric, and has produced the series of philosophers running from Hegel through Kierkegaard to Bergson, the Phenomenologists, and the Existentialists, while the English-speaking world continues to produce its formal logicians, nurturing no original theorists of becoming or of history comparable to Hegel or Bergson. (Toynbee is not a philosopher of history in the sense in which Hegel was, for, moving rather within the common pre-Christian circular or cyclic framework, his history tends to show that becoming is not really becoming at all but only ends where it began.) Speculation in the United States largely follows the British pattern. Nevertheless, from the beginning a sense of movement has been felt at every level of awareness on the American scene. One remembers Toqueville's admiration at the fact that even uneducated laborers in American shipyards were anxious to point out to him that American ships were built with little attention to permanence because, even in the America of his day, everyone was quite aware that the ships would be out of date long before their cheaply constructed hulls and tackle could get seriously out of order. In keeping with this awareness of movement, American thought itself is quite conscious in its own way of its own peculiar commitments to the future. If it is true that a strict Aristotelian formalism has been able to flourish in the United States as nowhere else today, it is also true that the American love of the frontier readily translates itself in more obscure ways from the geographical and social to the intellectual realm, sensitizing the American spirit to the frontiers which exist there.

V

If the fact of this translation, as it affects Catholics, is not very clearly or urgently apprehended by what we may call the general well informed Catholic consciousness, nevertheless it is registered by this consciousness in quite discernible ways.

The first half of the twentieth century will doubtless go down in history as the age when American Catholics were specializing in symbols of frontier or borderline operations. Their idols (the word is hardly too strong) include not only figures such as Chesterton, Waugh, Greene, Mrs. Clare Boothe Luce, and numbers of converted Communists and other converts who have appeared in England and the United States to testify to the religio-intellectual charge at the borderline between the Church and her surroundings, as well as similar figures in France—Péguy, Bloy, Ernest Psichari, and the like—but most especially two Europeans who have been first borrowed and more recently simply annexed by the English-speaking Catholics of North America, MM. Gilson and Maritain.

There can be little doubt that Professor Gilson has been sponsored by American Catholics not only out of admiration for his superb scholarship, but also out of some deep-felt emotional need. American Catholics commonly think of M. Gilson simply as a Thomist, but the author of *Thomism* himself has credited much of his interest in philosophy and inspiration to Bergson; and Bergson's sense of history, of a present which is and has always been the frontier where the past moves into the future, is undoubtedly one of the things which give M. Gilson his appeal to the contemporary American Catholic mind. For this mind, Gilson helps symbolically to endow even the reputed static qualities of the Middle Ages, and with them the similar qualities imputed (mistakenly) by Americans to Europe in general, with the sense of movement in history so congenial to the American sensibility.

As a symbol, M. Gilson affects the American Catholic mind apparently well below the threshold of consciousness, for he himself appears much more explicitly aware of the necessity of establishing a dialogue between the Faith and America and more inclined explicitly to view his own work as contributing to this dialogue than are his own American backers. So far as I have observed, American Catholics seem quite unaware that the title of M. Gilson's Harvard lectures in honor of their fellow American William James which they so widely read, *The Unity of Philosophical Experience,* is a take-off and commentary on the title of an earlier series of Gifford Lectures by William James himself, *The Varieties of Religious Experience.* It is fascinating to note that in this exchange of views—at a distance of some years—it is James whose sense of history was not very compelling and who studies the various manifestations of drives common to all, or many individuals, focusing on an an-historical diversity, whereas Gilson focuses on the unity evinced within movement or history, and thus gives comfort to the American Catholic unconscious in its own orientation toward movement.

The other favorite symbol of borderline activity, Professor Maritain, has been sponsored even more than Professor Gilson in the United States, where he is now more eminent than in his own country. Emerging from the same European-medieval context as Gilson, and thus giving American Catholics the assurance of continuity with the past that they need, Maritain puts the American Catholic ethos in contact less with the movement of history than with something else in its surroundings: the post-Newtonian scientific developments of a generation or two ago. It may fairly be said that he predigested these developments for American Catholic consumption. On the whole, his work in this field has been more widely attended to in America than his own more valuable work on Church-state relationships, which has had to compete with the parallel work of an American Jesuit, Father John Courtney Murray.

VI

The task of bringing the Catholic mind into fertile intellectual contact with America has been complicated by the involved and painful adjustment of this mind to romanticism, and that not only in art and literature—here the adjustment came rather easily to the Catholic sensibility—but in the realm of intellect itself.

The age of romanticism was marked by its own real and distinctive intellectual achievement. The earlier, the preromantic ages had labored to conceive knowledges which were as explicit and clear as possible, so that intellectual developments from antiquity through the age of rationalism represent in the large a movement from the mythological or cryptically symbolic interpretation of reality toward greater abstraction and more clear-cut formalism. This was as it should have been, for such a movement is the characteristic movement demanded by explanation and science.

Indeed, romanticism, although it moved in somewhat the opposite direction, was itself impossible except after such developments. Man needed a pretty full-blown science and rational philosophy and the feeling these engendered of some mastery over the universe before he could afford to own to himself the limitations of his knowledge. The romantic age marked, among other things, the acknowledgment in some sort of these limitations and a deliberate plunge back into the obscurity of symbolic as against abstract awarenesses. With the romantic age, man put aside to some extent his forms and abstractions to fumble again with the great mass of undigested impressions which resisted formalization. This sort of thing had been done before—in a sense had always been going on in the cabala and other forms of occultism, in mystical theology, and elsewhere—but never before had it been done so deliberately or on so large a scale. With romanticism, the unclassified and apparently unclassifiable aspects of reality, which included all the depths of immediate experience, became interesting to the whole world.

Not that preceding ages prided themselves in becoming rigid and unreal and abstractly remote in their intellectual activity. They felt their pursuit of formalism to be a fascinating pursuit of reality, as indeed it was up to a point. At its best, romanticism never questioned the preromantic, rationalist, intellectual performance for what it undoubtedly achieved. It merely made evident the limitations of the achievement to a degree unrealized in earlier times. The preromantic intellect had pursued light and had sought to illuminate the darkness with which man was surrounded. But it had not eliminated the darkness. With the romantic age came the acknowledgment of the fact that the darkness could never be effectively done away with, and the determination to face the dark as dark. From this time on, it becomes increasingly possible to talk about what is acknowledged to be obscure and intellectually recalcitrant. Coleridgean speculation, terminating in work such as Bergson's, comes into its own. Interest in the clearer forms of being is supplemented, or even replaced, by interest in mystery as such and in the vagaries of becoming.

Intellectual romanticism thus described has left a permanent mark on the Western mind, forcing adjustments not yet completed. It has discovered evolution and the fascinations of the history of thought. There is no doubt that one of the functions of scholars such as MM. Gilson and Maritain, both of whom propose an understanding of reality which, however unyielding in its rationality, is exceedingly respectful to the counterclaims of evolution and history, has been to import into the United States an adjustment to this intellectual romanticism already worked out, at least in its larger aspects, in Europe.

The United States was conceived and cradled in the Age of Reason as no European country had ever been. The intellectual tradition of the early Colonies was rife with "logic," which asserts itself not only in the rationalism of a Jefferson, but even more among the Puritans, as well as among later Evangelicals such as the Methodists, who, like the Puritans, were products of the logical tradition typified by Peter Ramus.

Not only the United States, but the Church herself in the United States has important relationships with this tradition. For here the Church was, as in no European country, formed by the post-Tridentine seminary training which had been conceived within the scientizing framework inherited by the Renaissance from the medieval university and subtly transmuted by the eighteenth century into "reason." The Catholic sensibility in the United States was given its characteristic orientations largely by the catechism, a product of Trent, rather than by the complex agglomerate of pre-Christian social customs and observances made over in accordance with Christian teaching such as one finds in European Catholic history or in that of Latin America. This is not to say that the American Catholic sensibility was not influenced by ritual and custom or that the older European Catholic sensibility was insensitive to dogma. It is merely to say that in the complex of abstract statement and ritual observance which defines Catholic teaching and determines its relation to the natural world, the American Catholic sensibility is more at home with the abstract code.

Ritual observances bind to time and space. And in a nation come into being "on the move" and conserved by telecommunication and airplanes, the whole psychological framework relating man to time and space is radically new. Thus the religious procession plays a decidedly minor role in the ethos of American Catholicism, and it has frequently been pointed out that there is practically no tradition of *local* saints or devotions (outside the spheres of French and Spanish cultural influences): the American Catholic's devotions are typically to the individual members of the Holy Family, which, like his own family, he regards as transportable, or, more specifically, often to Christ in the Blessed Sacrament, present around the world. These are devotions which he and his fathers have learned and fostered largely through the abstract code of their catechism. The resulting religious sensibility, at least up to now, is symbolically and artistically impoverished and unproductive in its abstractness, but it is remarkably orthodox, for it is based on an approach to the Faith which is about as scientized and standardized as an approach to what transcends reason can well be.

Nevertheless, if the United States was cradled in the repose of rationalism, it matured in the nineteenth century world filled with the sense of movement (which included and terminated in a sense of history) marking romanticism and postromanticism. But because of his double charge of "reason," one national and the other religious, the American Catholic has been exceedingly slow to register the romantic emphasis. He has in many ways reacted more slowly than the European Catholic because of his American rationalism, and more slowly than other Americans because of his Catholic rationalism. This is one reason why the Church in America is more legalistic in performance and more formalistic in general intellectual outlook than anywhere else in the world—with the possible exception of the Iberian peninsula. Interest in outdoor nature, a romantic interest so characteristic of the English-speaking world that even in Ireland Jesuit bird watchers publish notes in the national Jesuit monthly, is still viewed without enthusiasm in American Catholic circles, where manifestations of this interest are at best tolerated.

This fact is manifest in orientation not only at the scientific level but also at the level of practical sociology. Scouting, for example—in its various forms certainly a product of romanticism—was accepted by American Catholics with great reluctance, and then chiefly for negative reasons—to keep Catholic youth away from troops operated under non-Catholic sponsorship. The American Catholic, like all Americans, enjoys scenery. But he is not a promoter of the Great Outdoors which to him, in some mysterious way, seems to have been turned over by its Creator to the Protestants.

The American Catholic's slowness in intellectually assimilating the romantic heritage has given his attitude toward his Faith an invaluable reasoned stability, but it has not always guaranteed the relevance of his apologetic to the American actuality. The difficulties here can be seen, for example, in connection with the American Catholic stress on the natural law, the law of reason, generated by the widespread conviction that what is wrong with the non-Catholic world generally is "relativism" or "subjectivism," and that for this reason any effective apologetic must concentrate in season and out on promulgating this law of reason, as a reassertion of immutable principles.

But shot into enemy territory whose topography is not too well understood, this kind of apologetic can miss its intended mark, or even ricochet. For, in the United States, stress on the natural law has often rather uniformly been stress on the "rights" which favor employers over employees—the so-called "right-to-work" laws of some American states, which are really "union-busting" laws seriously restricting the right to organize, show the bias often imparted to the notion of right. Asserting the rights of labor in the

United States has thus paradoxically, in point of historical fact, been often a matter of attacking those who based their case on the natural law, and this fact is connected with—although it by no means entirely explains—the late Oliver Wendell Holmes's suspicion of the natural law, the late Louis D. Brandeis's record of dissenting decisions on the Supreme Court, and Dr. Reinhold Niebuhr's persistent sharpshooting at the Catholic natural-law emphasis.

For, however we may wish the facts to have been, it has fallen out that the postromantic world, sensitized to patterns of development, and not the world of rationalism, devoted to fixity and stability, has been the world witnessing the progressive betterment of the condition of the working classes. This fact does not deny the importance, historical as well as theoretical, of natural-law speculation in implementing present-day interests and improvements, but it infinitely complicates the picture and suggests that the presence of the Church to the American intellectual can perhaps be strengthened by a more sensitive approach to non-Catholic American culture than that which can see nothing in it but undifferentiated relativism and/or subjectivism.

VII

The assimilation of romanticism by Catholic thought in the United States involves what this same assimilation involves elsewhere, that is, in great part the utilization of the findings of anthropology, psychological analysis, and paleontology—this last particularly for the evolutionary data which it now supplies in such abundance as prenotes to a history of material being in its mysterious sequences from the time of its creation in its relatively undifferentiated forms until the advent of man. In terms of this history, these three fields of anthropology, paleontology, and psychological analysis (with its "collective memory") are tending to merge, or at least to pool their findings in such a way as to provide the occasion for a great wealth of new metaphysical insights.

However, it must be admitted that, to date, the defensive mentality inherited from post-Reformation Catholicism and intensified in their predominantly Protestant surroundings has brought the Catholics of the United States, more than those elsewhere, to see these developments, and a great many others, as productive of nothing more than "difficulties," and hence as annoyances to be dealt with by being somehow demolished, rather than as exciting occasions for enriching their own understanding of the universe in the light of their faith. Fortunately, this defensive mentality is now being superseded by a more positive approach, which will probably continue to grow as the American Catholic mind grows in its sense of history—a sense, that is, which involves not simply an interest in facts and a moralistic theory that history "teaches lessons," but rather an insight into the process of becoming apprehended in its real and irreversible details as this process relates to metaphysics and to a whole *Weltanschauung*. After all, if certain species of being—the dinosaur or the pterodactyl—appear at a certain point in the evolution of material being and thereupon disappear *as species* never to reappear, we are face to face with a metaphysical problem concerning the significance of this special kind of foredoomed existence. And we now know that the story of material being—until we get to man—is a story of this sort of thing.

American Catholic thought need not necessarily concern itself specifically with dinosaurs or pterodactyls, but it seems unlikely that it can mature until it succeeds in dealing with America itself and America's particular place along the irreversible trajectory which history is describing. This is not to call for chauvinism or for a specialization in "Americanology" based on the belief that this country is called by God to lead the rest of a benighted world to salvation. In fact, one of the difficulties facing the Catholic sensibility in the United States is precisely the tendency of many Catholics to let their understanding of the United States be defined by something like such jingoism. The need for a Catholic appreciation of America in its historical setting arises not from the demands of patriotism but from the fact that one's intellectual maturity today is tied up with one's insight into and acceptance of one's own history in relation to the whole of history. The inability of Catholic culture in America to produce—with some few exceptions—anything in philosophy or theology other than textbooks is intimately connected with an inability of the culture to "find" itself intellectually in relation to the whole panorama of human, and Catholic, activity unfolding from creation till now and including the phenomenon of America in its sweep.

Moreover, while the United States has no mission, and no possibility, of making over the rest of the world into a kind of imitation of herself, nevertheless the fact remains that many of the more significant developments affecting world culture are at present concentrated in the United States in a special way, so that, to some extent, an understanding of the United States is necessary for an understanding of the direction being taken by the whole contemporary world. The obvious instances of such developments are those in the field of technology, but, I believe, at least equally important are those in the field of "human relations" or "personal relations." If American Catholic thought can address itself more and more to such developments in the real milieu in which it finds itself, bringing its attention explicitly to bear on the realities through which Revelation engages the America around it, real progress can be hoped for. Not a little progress can, indeed, already be reported: for example, in the work of the farseeing laymen engaged in publishing the periodical *Cross Currents*, or of those responsible for the book *Catholicism in America*, a collection of articles reprinted from the weekly *Commonweal;* or in the current orientation of the magazine *Thought* at Fordham University, or in the Institute for Social Order at Saint Louis University and its forward-looking publication *Social Order*.

If Catholic thought is to move further along these lines of contact with the American reality, what it needs is to envision a real Christian *mystique* of technology and science. That is, it needs to develop a real spiritual insight into technology and science which at least attempts to discover and discuss the philosophical and theological meaning of the technological and scientific trend which marks our age. It is certain that a mature understanding of this trend can never be arrived at until the American Catholic sensibility can transcend the impoverished frames of thought which can discern in post-Renaissance, or even in all postmedieval, developments nothing more than the progressive secularization and materialization of society. For only in certain ways is this age involved with the secular and material more than other ages. On the one hand, the Church as a whole is freer of secular (in the sense of direct political) influence than she has ever been in her history, and, on the other, this age is the age of victory over the tyranny of matter greater than the world has ever before known. Our present *concern* over becoming materialistic is something, after all, not only new but long overdue, and in this sense a real spiritual achievement of the twentieth century. In a similar way, this age, so often denounced as impersonal, has paid more explicit attention to the person than any other age in history. The philosophical movement known as personalism is a distinctive twentieth century product.

The problem of the American Catholic sensibility vis-à-vis the technological and scientific world is no doubt in great part liturgical. Perhaps what is ultimately needed is to augment our sacramentals with new ones. The older sacramentals—holy water, incense, the various blessings—represent in great part an assimilation and consecration by the Church of observances pagan or secular in origin and tied most often to nature symbolism. Our age—and in the United States perhaps more than in any other place to date—has overlaid the nature symbols in the human consciousness with symbols from the mechanical and commercial world. Advertisements, it has been frequently remarked, show how far the automobile has become psychologically a substitute for woman (wife or mother). Security has become associated with insurance policies more than with firesides. The aggressive man is faced with symbolic abstractions mechanistically processed, such as the "crushing" effect of "monopolies" or the "steamroller methods" of "big business," rather than with saber-toothed tigers and mastodons.

The later mechanico-commercial symbolism has not exactly displaced the earlier nature symbolism, but has rather effectively overlaid it. Balder may still die in every rotation of the seasons, but his death has curious complications since the world became steam heated and air conditioned.

In the face of these developments, although some hints may be found in a book such as *The Mass of the Future,* by the American liturgist Father Gerald Ellard, S.J., the precise direction which liturgical developments will take is very hard to predict, for the lively symbols which inhabit the American imagination—the Coca-Cola girl, Dagwood and Blondie, the voice of the laboratory, the Gallup poll, the Great Book, the real-estate business, the funeral parlor, the gadget, and so many other symbols of popular culture which interest the anthropologist—spring from psychological depths which the American Catholic mind has yet to explore in their religious implications. At the present stage, the American Catholic sensibility is often the victim of a kind of liturgical sluggishness, which leaves it quite unaware how far its own forms of thought are being controlled by the symbolism of the industrial world to which it affects a studied indifference. Often the same Catholics, lay and clerical, who refer without second thought to their "parish plant" where "a good Catholic product" is being "turned out" will resist to the last ditch any inclusion in church art of symbols referring to contemporary industrial or technological existence.

As a foundation for their own intellectual self-possession, Catholics in the United States need a *mystique* of more than technology and science. They need also a Christian *mystique* of such things as sports and lunch clubs—the two important avenues into the male world kept open by American Catholicism—and indeed a *mystique* of the whole social surface which is a property of life in the United States. This social surface is maintained in great part by the arts of communication in the peculiar and highly developed conditions in which these arts exist in the United States. Here what the ancient world knew as "rhetoric" or "oratory"—the art of swaying other men, conceived as more or less the crown of all education—long ago migrated from the faculties of languages into the university courses in commerce and finance, where it is taught under labels such as "advertising," or "copy writing," or "merchandizing" and "marketing" and "salesmanship." This twentieth century rhetoric, like all rhetoric, has a strong personalist torque—it has ultimately to face the problem of dealing with the individual as an individual—and has given rise to the American stress on personal relations and personnel problems and adjustments which has appeared as one of the great, and not entirely unsuccessful, compensatory efforts of a mechanistic civilization, grown self-conscious, to deal with its own peculiar shortcomings. American Catholics need a *mystique* of this peculiar American personalism, too. Catholic thought here could conceivably make a real intellectual contribution to the United States by bringing to bear on this area of personalist activity the phenomenological analysis closely connected with European personalism, except that American Catholic thought is even more uninformed about phenomenology than American non-Catholic thought is. But there are interesting signs that some American Catholic philosophers are becoming interested in phenomenology and even in dialogue as a condition and frame of philosophical thinking.

Catholics in the United States could well do with a *mystique,* too, of American optimism, which they have by now assimilated perhaps more thoroughly than their Protestant neighbors, the originators of the optimism. This American optimism is psychologically linked with the hopeful facing into the future which so far has marked the American mind. Such facing into the future can be naïve, but it has, or can have, profound relevance to the Catholic outlook. For the *restauratio* of all things in Christ, of which the Popes speak in recent encyclicals, is something which lies not behind but ahead. Although the Church transcends history in the sense that her mission is being fulfilled at all times, and although this mission is to restore all things to their Origin, nevertheless the restoration is effected in the future, not in the past. Creation returns to God not by retracing its steps, not by moving back toward

Christ at the intersection of the Old and the New and thence back through the Old, but rather by moving forward with Christ in the continued action of the Incarnation. Not only is a reverse movement impossible, but, looking back, one can assign no point at which the full *restauratio* was effected. The route of this return through the future is what chiefly sanctifies creation, for, as St. Thomas Aquinas views it, things go out from God by nature and return, not by nature, but through Christ, by what we would today call a supernatural route (although the term "supernatural" was, of course, not exploited by St. Thomas). At the end of this route, things are not at the same pass that they were at in the beginning, for at the end the supernaturalization is more complete, and the Church more perfect in her complement of souls.

There was a time at the turn of the century when the Catholic consciousness in America seemed on the point of taking explicit intellectual cognizance of the forward-looking habits endemic in the American state of mind. But the circumstances terminating in the letter, "Testem benevolentiae," of Leo XIII to Cardinal Gibbons, without effecting the condemnation of anything in the United States, abruptly killed off the dialogue between the Church and America which Hecker, Archbishop Ireland, Orestes Brownson, and others had initiated, and dealt a blow to American Catholic self-confidence from which the American Catholic mind has never effectively recovered. Since then, the American Catholic has lived the myth of America, but he has hardly dared to speculate as to its meaning in relation to his faith, or to the spiritual, interior life which this faith demands of him. Today, when our world perspectives are enlarging, so that America can be seen as part of the general movement of the human spirit through history, meaningful in terms of the over-all trajectory of history, should the American Catholic intellectual succeed in returning to his roots in his own American world, he will doubtless better succeed in thinking through his connections with the rest of mankind, and in living out his own tiny share of the total life of Christ.

Father Walter J. Ong, S.J. — editor of *Darwin's Vision and Christian Perspectives* and author of *American Catholic Crossroads* — analyzes the unique character of Catholicism in the United States and shows its adaptability to the atmosphere of the American Community in

FRONTIERS IN AMERICAN CATHOLICISM

Essays on Ideology and Culture

Father Ong's insights into the philosophical and theological meanings of our age provide a basis for more effective social action and intellectual maturity. In defining a Christian humanism capable of assimilating technology, he pays tribute to this age, so often denounced as impersonal. Actually it "has paid more explicit attention to the person than any other age in history"; and the philosophical movement known as personalism he regards as a "distinctive twentieth century product." With a keen awareness of what is vital for American Catholics, the author points out new fields of thought that challenge the Church in America — ones that are comparable to the experience of the frontier, the spirit of enterprise, exploration, and expansion.

"Thoughtful evaluation of American Catholicism's position *vis-à-vis* the modern intellectual world. This volume deserves wide reading and serious appraisal."

— *America*

Cover design by The Strimbans